# A House Divided

## The Lives of
## Ulysses S. Grant
## and
## Robert E. Lee

# A House Divided

## The Lives of
## Ulysses S. Grant
### and
## Robert E. Lee

Jules Archer

**SCHOLASTIC
HARDCOVER**

Scholastic Inc.
New York

**Picture Credits**

**Pictures 1-1, 1-2, 1-3, 1-10, 2-9 and 2-10:** National Archives.
**Pictures 1-9, 1-11, 2-3, 2-4, 2-6 and 2-7:** Library of Congress.
**Pictures 1-4, 1-6, 1-12, 2-1 and 2-8:** The Bettmann Archives.
**Pictures 1-5, 1-8, 2-2, 2-5, 2-11, and 2-12:** Illinois State Historical
Library.
**Picture 1-7:** Culver Pictures, Inc.

Library of Congress Cataloging-in-Publication Data
Archer, Jules.
A house divided : the lives of Ulysses S. Grant and Robert E. Lee
/ by Jules Archer.
p.    cm.
Includes bibliographical references (p.   ) and index.
ISBN 0-590-48325-0
1. United States—History—Civil War, 1861–1865—Biography—Juvenile
literature.  2. Grant, Ulysses S. (Ulysses Simpson), 1822–1885—Juvenile
literature.  3. Lee, Robert E. (Robert Edward), 1807–1870—Juvenile
literature.  4. Generals—United States—Biography—Juvenile literature.
5. Generals—Confederate States of America—Biography—Juvenile
literature.  6. United States. Army—Biography—Juvenile literature.
7. Confederate States of America. Army—Biography—Juvenile literature.
I. Title.
E467.A73   1995
973.7'092'2—dc20
[B]                                                                    93-38886
                                                                          CIP
12 11 10 9 8 7 6 5 4 3 2 1              5 6 7 8 9 0/0 9/9

Printed in the U.S.A.                                    37

First Scholastic printing, January 1995

*To my newest grandchildren*
*Zoe Alena and Nikkita Paige Archer*
*and*
*Dr. Sue Hand Archer*

# Contents

# 1

# Young Lee

Robert Edward Lee was born on January 19, 1807, in a Virginia mansion, Stratford Hall, on the Potomac River in Westmoreland County. Another Virginian was president at the time — Thomas Jefferson.

Robert was the fifth child and youngest son of Henry Lee and Ann Hill Carter Lee, who was the daughter of a rich plantation owner. His father, a hero of the American Revolution, had been nicknamed "Light-Horse Harry" for his swift cavalry attacks against the British. Henry Lee, a favorite of George Washington's, was governor of Virginia from 1791 to 1794.

Robert grew up reminded constantly of his father's fame. He was also in awe of George Washington, who had praised Robert's father for displaying "a remarkable degree of prudence, enterprise and bravery."

But Henry Lee had plunged from the heights to the depths, seeking his fortune in reckless speculations that ruined him. Bankrupt and in debt, he was thrown in jail twice. He was imprisoned a third time for opposing the War of 1812, and was badly hurt when an angry mob stormed the jail to seize him.

Penniless, broken in body and spirit, Henry Lee, never to return, sailed off to the West Indies, leaving his family. Robert never really knew his father, who was absent most of the time, and who died when Robert was only eleven.

Robert was three when his mother moved the family to Alexandria, Virginia, to be closer to relatives and good schools for children. Robert found the city exciting. He loved to sit at the docks and watch foreign ships from all over the world collect Virginia's bales of cotton and tobacco.

Robert had an early love of horses. Attending horse markets, he learned how to judge good mounts. He also enjoyed swimming, ice-skating, fishing, and duck hunting.

Like many boys his age, Robert had a temper that sometimes led him into fights. He strove to keep it under control, especially in later years, when he wanted to present a calm, dignified appearance. If he did lose his temper, he hastily sought to make amends to the person scolded. His disposition was usually amiable and he could never hold a grudge.

He was only seven when the War of 1812, which his father opposed, brought invading British warships into the Potomac River.

Forts below Alexandria were attacked. When the

city surrendered, redcoats swarmed over its streets. Robert could see smoke rising from the capital, which the British had set on fire. This frightening experience gave him his first taste of the kind of war his father and Washington had fought.

His mother often took Robert and the other Lee children to her family estate, a plantation called Shirley. Here he would watch a blacksmith shoe horses, millers grind grain into flour, and carpenters make furniture. The Carter family maintained its own schools, and Robert attended his first class at age nine. A serious student, he excelled in all his studies. He also proved to be a fine athlete, rider, boxer, and fencer.

The Carter family helped give Robert an aristocratic upbringing, making him something of a snob in the process. But he didn't forget the fact that he, his mother, and his brothers and sisters were really poor relations at the Shirley plantation. He knew that his family owned none of the fine things made available to them; that in actuality they depended on Carter family charity.

Overhearing discussions of his father's disgrace, Robert burned with humiliation. He sought to make up for it by behaving like a perfect gentleman at all times. Later, his dignified bearing made others assume that he had been born an aristocrat.

By the time news of his father's death reached the Lee family, Robert's brothers and older sister had left the Shirley plantation. His widowed mother, her hopes for an eventual reunion with her husband shattered, fell seriously ill.

Eleven-year-old Robert took upon his shoulders the role of man of the house. Adoring his mother, he watched over her vigilantly, did the marketing, attended to household chores, looked after the horses, and paid the bills. He also took his mother for daily carriage rides, cheered her with lighthearted talk, read to her, and in every way demonstrated a great sense of compassion and responsibility.

Beginning at age twelve, he attended the free Alexandria Academy for three years. When he graduated, his mother could not afford to send him to college. The solution was a free higher education at West Point. A career in the military appealed to Robert, since he aspired to imitate the heroic example of Light-Horse Harry Lee in the American Revolution.

He hoped that in time his own military achievements would make Virginia once more proud of the Lee name, erasing the memory of his father's disgrace.

His teachers provided glowing reports, praising Robert's character, intellect, studiousness, high morals, and gentlemanly bearing. These impressed five senators and three representatives, whose recommendations won him an appointment to West

Point. Before leaving for the academy Robert took a year of preparatory studies in mathematics.

"He was a most exemplary pupil in every respect," his instructor wrote later. "He was never behind time at his studies; never failed in a single recitation; was perfectly observant of the rules and regulations of the institution; was gentlemanly, unobstructive and respectful in all his deportment to teachers and his fellow students." He was, in fact, a little too well-behaved for the other students, who enjoyed a little mischief.

In July 1825 eighteen-year-old Robert entered West Point at the same time Abraham Lincoln was trying to educate himself in the backwoods of Indiana, and three-year-old Ulysses S. Grant was toddling around his father's farm in Ohio.

Robert enjoyed the challenge of the Point's strenuous hours of daily drill, the strict military regulations, and the intense competition of other cadets. Aware that his future in the military depended upon his success at the academy, he strove to become a model cadet. When classmates got drunk and fired off pistols in the barracks, Robert was not among them.

At the end of his plebe year he was awarded the highest honor of his class with an appointment as staff sergeant of the cadet corps. He was also made an assistant professor of mathematics. Robert became the first cadet at West Point to receive absolutely no demerits.

When he arrived home on furlough at the end of his second year, he found his mother an invalid, dying of a terminal illness. Her face lit up at the sight of the dashing, handsome figure her son cut in his gray cadet uniform.

His Carter girl cousins were equally intrigued, and sought his company. Two confessed that they were smitten by Lee's "manly beauty and fine manners." He was swept up in riding parties, picnics, wagon rides, moonlight dances, and boating excursions. His social graces grew even more polished.

In Lee's last year at the Point, he was appointed corps adjutant, a post given the cadet with the finest military bearing and best record on the drill ground.

Fellow cadet and Virginia friend Joe Johnston, later to become a general serving under Lee in the Civil War, wrote, "We had the same intimate associates, who thought as I did, that no other youth or man so united the qualities that win warm friendship and command high respect."

In 1829 Lee graduated as a second lieutenant in the corps of engineers. He was second in his class. Rushing home to the bedside of his dying mother, he became a full-time nurse for her. Whenever he left her room, her gaze would follow him, and she would watch the door steadily until his return.

When she died, Lee felt a crushing grief that overcame him even forty years later upon returning to the same room.

On November 1, 1829, he arrived at his first post, bleak Cockspur Island, Georgia. Here he assisted in building a fort.

On a furlough next year he returned to Virginia, where he courted a distant cousin and childhood playmate, Mary Custis, the great-granddaughter of Martha Washington. She had previously turned down a proposal from Tennessee frontiersman Sam Houston. In 1830 slim, dark-eyed Mary wrote a friend, "I am engaged to one to whom I have been long attached — Robert Lee."

Plans were made for the wedding the next spring when Lee was transferred to Fort Monroe, Virginia. Ever the fussy dandy, Lee wrote his brother Carter in New York, "I believe I will wear my uniform coat on the important night & therefore *white* pantaloons must be in character. . . . Let the material of all be the best & don't let him charge too much."

On a second lieutenant's salary, Lee was still the poor relative, and was now more conscious than ever of presenting an elegant appearance.

Mary Custis was a practical choice for Lee, who was aware that his rather plain, dark-haired bride was sole heiress to a large fortune. She also reminded him of the mother he had greatly loved. Sharing his fondness for riding and reading, Mary

Custis seemed to Lee most compatible as a life companion and mother for his children, of which there were to be seven.

Finally, her family relationship to his hero, George Washington, added to the prestige of the marriage.

When the wedding date was set, Lee wrote Carter, "I begin to feel right *funny* when I count my days. . . . Can you come on to see it done? . . . . I am told there are to be *six* pretty Brides maids . . . & you could have some fine kissing. For you know what a fellow you are at these weddings."

Mary's father, George Washington Parke Custis, was not too happy about his daughter marrying the penniless son of the disgraced Henry Lee, but he was gradually won over. The wedding took place on June 30, 1831, at the Custis plantation called Arlington on the banks of the Potomac.

On Lee's honeymoon he took the time to write his army captain, revealing, "The Parson had a few words to say, though he dwelt upon them as if he had been reading my Death warrant. . . . I felt 'bold as a sheep' & was surprised at my want of Romance in so great a degree as not to feel more excited."

If Mary Custis loved Lee, it was obvious that for him their union was largely a marriage of convenience. Nevertheless, as part of his code of honor, he always remained a loyal husband.

During Lee's many assignments to different posts, Mary often could not accompany him. Her loneliness was relieved by their steadily increasing family and, whenever Lee was home, he proved a devoted and doting father.

Duty, however, always came before Lee's personal concerns. Once when Mary was sick, she wrote urging him to return from Michigan, where he had been sent to settle a boundary dispute with Ohio.

"Why do you urge my *immediate* return," he replied testily, "and tempt me in the *strongest* manner, to endeavor to get excused from the performance of a duty, imposed on me by my profession, for the pure gratification of my private feelings? . . . . I must not consent to do aught that would lower me in your eyes, my own & that of others."

In his letters Lee sometimes showed a priggishness, a self-importance and superiority that some found annoying.

Despite his aristocratic manner, Lee demonstrated a surprising democratic instinct for an army officer. Sent to St. Louis on an army construction job, he joined civilian workers every morning at sunrise, working beside them under a blazing sun. He shared the same rations and ate with them.

"He was one with whom nobody ever wished or ventured to take a liberty," observed a lieutenant who worked with him, "though kind and generous to his subordinates, admired by all women, and respected by all men."

Wherever he was posted, Lee enjoyed the attention of women. Aware of it, Mary wrote a friend wryly, "No one enjoyed the society of ladies more than himself. It seemed the greatest recreation in his toilsome life."

No scandal, however, ever touched Lee. He always remained a faithful husband and affectionate father.

As a father he never forgot the hurt his own father's downfall had inflicted upon him as a boy. Once while at home walking in the snow with Lee's oldest son, Curtis, the boy fell behind. Turning, Lee was amused to see his son taking long strides to fit in his father's tracks.

"When I saw this," Lee told a friend, "I said to myself, 'It behooves me to walk very straight when this fellow is already following in my tracks!' " He would not inflict upon his children the sorrow his father's mistakes had caused him.

In June 1844 Lee was selected by President John Tyler to serve on a board supervising West Point examinations. The board was headed by fellow Virginian Winfield Scott, who was now commanding general of the U.S. army. During this stint, Lee grew well acquainted with Scott, who was greatly impressed with Lee's character, ability, and military bearing.

General Scott never imagined that he and the admirable young lieutenant were destined to become deadly enemies.

# 2

# Young Grant

Galloping his horse one day to court Julia Dent, young Ulysses S. Grant found that heavy rains had swollen the creek he needed to cross to overflowing.

The current was swift and dangerous.

"One of my superstitions," he wrote later, "had always been when I started to go anywhere, or to do anything, not to turn back, or stop until the thing intended was accomplished. . . . So I struck into the stream, and in an instant the horse was swimming and I being carried down by the current. I headed the horse towards the other bank and soon reached it, wet through and without other clothes. I went on, however, to my destination."

Grant's determination to plunge ahead, despite all obstacles, until he reached his goal, was to pose a challenge to General Robert E. Lee during their clash in the Civil War twenty years later.

Hiram Ulysses Grant was born at Point Pleasant, Ohio, on April 27, 1822, fifteen years after Lee, the Virginian destined to become his greatest adversary.

Called Lyss as a boy, he was renamed Ulysses S.

Grant when a congressman filled out his application for West Point and erroneously dropped the Hiram, giving him the middle initial "S" instead for his mother's maiden name, Simpson. Ulysses actually preferred the name because the initials of his birth name spelled "HUG," provoking teasing by schoolmates, who also mocked him by calling him "Useless." Early taunts bothered the sensitive boy, tending to make him something of a loner.

Little is known of Grant's mother. A handsome, dark-haired, slender Pennsylvania woman from a well-educated family, she was extremely shy, reserved, and silent. Her family shielded her from the public for reasons never revealed. Grant apparently never felt close to her. In Grant's autobiography all he writes about her is that "in June 1821 my father, Jesse R. Grant, married Hannah Simpson." All his references to his parentage are limited to his father. When he became president for eight years, not once did his mother visit him in the White House.

Grant's father Jesse was born in Pennsylvania, but as a youngster moved to Kentucky. He left that state, explaining, "I would not own slaves and I would not live where there were slaves." Opening a tannery in Georgetown, Ohio, he worked hard to give his six children the education denied him. He had to pay for their schooling, since no schools were free.

"I was not studious in habit," Ulysses acknowledged, "and probably did not make progress enough to compensate for the outlay for board and tuition." He suffered punishment for his shortcomings as a scholar, admitting, "The rod was freely used there, and I was not exempt from its influence."

Ulysses grew up in Georgetown, a little country town in southern Ohio with a courthouse square but no courthouse. He had five younger siblings — Samuel Simpson, Clara Rachel, Virginia Paine (Jennie), Orvil Lynch, and Mary Frances.

The quiet, blue-eyed boy with fair skin and auburn hair was required to help his father in the tannery. Ulysses hated it for its awful smells and bloodstained hides. As a result he could only eat meat when it was cooked to a cinder, because the sight of blood destroyed his appetite — an ironic handicap for a future warrior. Ulysses was much happier hauling wood and doing farm chores, especially working with horses, all of which he did as early as age seven.

As a child he exhibited two traits that were to prove his undoing as an adult — a naive trust in people and a lack of business sense. At eight he yearned for a colt owned by a man named Ralston who wanted twenty-five dollars for it. He told Ralston, "Papa says I may offer you twenty dollars for the colt, but if you won't take that, I am to offer twenty-two fifty, and if you won't take that, to give you twenty-five."

Not surprisingly, he had to pay twenty-five dollars for the colt.

This lack of guile was also to characterize his business dealings as a man, invariably ending in financial disaster.

At eleven Ulysses was handling horses, plowing, farming, hauling, and sawing firewood even while attending school. As a reward his father permitted him to go fishing, swim in a creek a mile away, visit his grandfather in the adjoining county by horseback, ice-skate, and ride a horse-drawn sleigh in wintertime.

"I had as many privileges as any boy in the village," he recalled, "and probably more than most of them. I have no recollection of ever having been punished at home by scolding or the rod." In school, however, he was not spared his teacher's long beech switch over his backside, a common schoolhouse practice in those days.

His father, despairing of making a tanner out of Ulysses, decided his son might have a better future in the military. Jesse Grant sought an appointment for him to West Point, which would at least provide free education.

For Grant, West Point offered an escape from the tannery, as well as an opportunity to travel and see the world outside Ohio. But he feared the academy's rigid requirements.

He was surprised when he easily passed the entrance exam in 1839. Nevertheless he sighed later,

"A military life had no charms for me, and I had not the faintest idea of staying in the army even if I should be graduated, which I did not expect."

A reluctant student, he spent more time reading novels than textbooks. Too small to excel at any West Point sport, he also hated military discipline. He constantly received demerits for sloppy dress, unmilitary posture, an inability to march in step, and lateness to class. His disinterest in looking soldierly would later be reflected in his rumpled appearance as a general.

In addition to his distaste for the spit-and-polish of Point life, he found it a struggle to keep up with his studies.

Grant's greatest pleasure at the Point was horsemanship. His high jump record remained unbeaten for twenty-five years. But his overall academy record was so bad that after being promoted temporarily to the rank of sergeant, he was demoted to private for his fourth year. One reason may have been his frequenting an off-limits local bar. Through a great deal of his life Grant relied on liquor for a lift when he felt depressed.

Several cadets who attended the Point at the same time were to cross his path later in the Civil War. They included William Tecumseh Sherman, a senior when Grant was a freshman, and George B. McClellan, a freshman when Grant was a senior.

Despite Grant's aversion to his life at the Point, he appreciated its importance to him. "I would not go away on any account," he wrote a cousin. "If a man graduates here, he is safe for life, let him go where he will."

When he graduated in 1843 Grant stood twenty-first in a class of thirty-nine, and one hundred and fifty-eighth in conduct among the Academy's two hundred twenty-three cadets. It was a dismal showing compared to Lee's record fifteen years earlier.

Applying for the cavalry he was made a second lieutenant in the infantry instead. After ordering an officer's uniform, he waited for it impatiently so that he could swagger in it back home. "I probably wanted my old schoolmates, particularly the girls, to see me in it," he recalled.

Heading home on horseback, he sought to present an imposing appearance. He was embarrassed when he was teased, first by a shoeshine boy, then by a stable hand.

"The conceit was knocked out of me," he wrote. "[It] gave me a distaste for military uniforms that I never recovered from." That was why, during the Civil War, the commander-in-chief of the Union army invariably dressed like a sloppy private.

Grant was assigned to the 4th U.S. Infantry at Jefferson Barracks, near St. Louis, Missouri, along with his fourth-year Point roommate, Frederick Dent. He told Dent that after his obligatory tour of duty, he intended to resign from the army and seek a career as a college professor. His qualifications were questionable, however. In a letter he wrote to Dent's sister Julia, in just one paragraph he had two misspellings — "shure" and "influance."

Grant spent a lot of his free time at the Dent family home, where he courted Julia Dent, an ardent young horsewoman. Julia had plain features, an eye defect, a thick neck, and a stumpy figure. Grant admired her amiable disposition and tact. She also shared his love of horses.

"Such delightful rides we used to take," Julia recalled.

They became engaged in May 1844, but did not marry until four years later because of Grant's frequent changes of post.

When President James Polk plotted to annex Texas, which American settlers had torn away from Mexico, Grant's regiment was sent to the western border of Louisiana in 1845.

Grant was totally opposed to the annexation of Texas, as was then-congressman Abraham Lincoln. "[I] regard the war which resulted," Grant wrote later, "as one of the most unjust ever waged by a stronger against a weaker nation . . . to acquire additional territory." He was under no illusions about the hypocrisy of President Polk in sending U.S. troops to the Mexican border.

"We were sent to provoke a fight," he wrote, "but it was essential that Mexico should commence it . . . Mexico showing no willingness to come to the Nueces River to drive the invaders from her soil, it became necessary for the 'invaders' to approach to within a convenient distance to be struck.''

Despite his cynicism, Grant's West Point training did not allow him to think of disobeying commands to fight the Mexicans.

# 3

# Gallantry Under Fire

When the Mexican War broke out, Robert E. Lee was anxious to join the army of General Zachary Taylor, a fourth cousin, in Texas. Instead he was posted at Fort Hamilton to construct fortifications in New York harbor. Bored with routine army engineering, Lee knew that the engineers who took part in the Mexican War would advance far more swiftly than those who did not.

He was happy when, on August 19, 1846, he was ordered to report to Brigadier General John E. Wool in Texas for service in Mexico. Lee was joined by another West Pointer in the engineers, Lieutenant Pierre Beauregard, who was later to make history with Lee in the Civil War.

Lee saw coming battles as his opportunity to distinguish himself like Light-Horse Harry Lee. Yet, like Grant, he was cynical about the necessity or justification of going to war against Mexico. "It is true that we have bullied her," he wrote. "For that I am ashamed."

On March 24, 1847, Lee personally directed a battery of six guns firing on Vera Cruz, and came under answering shellfire for the first time in his life. He felt conflicted about ordering his men to bombard the city.

"Their fire was terrific," he wrote. " . . . . It was awful! My heart bled for the inhabitants. The soldiers I did not care so much for, but it was terrible to think of the women & children." As his battery rained death upon the city's civilians, Lee could not help visualizing Mary and his own children.

After a relentless three-day bombardment, the surrounded defenders of Vera Cruz surrendered to General Scott.

At Cerro Gordo, Lee was chosen to lead General David Twiggs's division on a rugged march over ravine walls so steep cannon had to be hauled up by rope. Guiding the division through ravines and huge boulders, Lee came under fierce enemy fire.

"The musket balls and grape were whistling over my head in a perfect shower," he wrote his fifteen-year-old son Curtis afterwards. "I thought of you, my dear Curtis, and wondered . . . where I could put you, if with me, to be safe. I was truly thankful you were at school."

When Scott's forces attacked Cerro Gordo, supported by Lee's artillery, the Mexicans broke and fled. Many were killed, wounded, or captured. The victory opened the way to invading Mexico City.

"The papers cannot tell you," Lee wrote home, "what a terrible sight a field of battle is."

In General Scott's official report of the battle of Cerro Gordo, he wrote, "I am compelled to make special mention of the services of Captain R.E. Lee, Engineer.''

For ''gallantry and meritorious conduct,'' Lee was made a major. His pluck and daring were the talk of the American forces in Mexico, reaching the ears of Lieutenant Ulysses S. Grant.

As Scott's army advanced in August, the Mexicans established a powerful camp on heights near Contreras, blocking passage by the Americans. Lee developed battle plans that led to a victory in what became known as the Battle of Contreras.

A delighted Scott then let it be known that he considered Lee his most promising junior officer, as well as ''the greatest military genius in America.''

Lee's tactics also helped Scott capture Curubusco. He was once more given a field promotion, becoming a lieutenant colonel. General Persifor Smith praised his ''soundness of judgment and his personal daring.''

Yet in keeping with his idea of gentlemanly modesty, when Lee wrote home he barely mentioned the honors he had won. He merely told Mary, ''I endeavored to give thanks to our Heavenly Father . . . for his preservation of me through all the dangers I have passed.''

Lee also played a daring role in the capture of Chapultepec, the last stronghold before Mexico City. So weary he could barely stay in the saddle, he was wounded riding through enemy fire, but continued to guide the attacking American forces.

Lee was present as the American flag was raised over Chapultepec Palace. For his bravery, Scott promoted him again, to a full colonel, a rank he held for the rest of the war.

The Treaty of Guadalupe Hidalgo was signed on February 2, 1848. It forced Mexico to relinquish Texas, cede New Mexico and California, and territory that included the present states of Arizona, Nevada, Utah, and parts of New Mexico, Colorado, and Wyoming. Thus ended Robert E. Lee's twenty months of war experience. It had taught him valuable lessons that he was to apply in the coming war between the states.

When Lee finally returned home, he was startled at how much older and different his children looked. He even made the mistake of hugging a neighbor's boy, thinking that the boy was his son Robert.

Back from the war, Lee was looked upon as a dashing Southern gentleman, chivalrous, courteous, dignified. Regarded with respect and admiration by men and women alike, he was now somewhat humorless and austere, possibly as a result of his close brushes with death in Mexico.

Assigned to Baltimore in 1848, he supervised construction of Fort Carroll for nearly four years, a humdrum task after the excitement of the Mexican War.

Lee tried to discourage his sons from entering the military. "I can advise no young man to enter the Army," he declared. "The same application, the same self denial, the same endurance in any other profession, will advance him faster and farther." Despite his advice, all of his sons sought to become military men like their father. General Scott's recommendation won Lee's son Curtis admission to West Point in 1850.

In 1852 Lee was appointed superintendent of the academy, where he remained for three years. Here he made a deep impression on a whole generation of army officers, some of whom later served with him in the Confederate army.

Lee raised the Point's academic standards, improved its facilities, and lengthened its program from four to five years. He had the cooperation of Jefferson Davis, who was now Secretary of War in the administration of President Franklin Pierce.

When Indian fighting broke out on the plains, Davis won Pierce's permission to raise two new regiments in 1855. That April Lee was ordered to Fort Cooper, Texas, to take his first field command as a peacetime lieutenant colonel, which was now his regular peacetime rank, of the 2nd Cavalry.

Instead of fighting Indians at Fort Cooper, Lee was bored, with no distractions except tarantulas and rattlesnakes.

"Fighting is the easiest part of a soldier's duty," he told a friend. "It is the watching, waiting, laboring, starving, freezing, wilting, exposures and privations that is so wearing to the body and trying to the mind."

In Texas Lee was absorbed by news of increasing clashes between abolitionists and slave-owners in many states. He wrote Mary, "In this enlightened age, there are few, I believe, but what will acknowledge that slavery as an institution is a moral and political evil in any Country."

Yet he viewed the abolitionists as dangerous radicals who would cause clashes between the North and South. Emancipation of the slaves, he chose to believe, would take place sooner through the kindness of slave-owners influenced by Christianity. That this hadn't happened in the over three hundred years since the slaves had been brought to America's shores made Lee's assumption highly unlikely, and an excuse for keeping slavery in place.

When Lee's father-in-law died in October, Lee obtained a leave of absence to run the estate. In the sumptuous Arlington mansion, the Lees entertained generously, welcoming waves of aunts, uncles, cousins, friends, and even strangers. In the spirit of Virginia hospitality, all guests, expected or not, were made to feel at home. Every morning Lee would gather rosebuds and place one on the plate of each woman guest before she came to breakfast.

*The New York Tribune* reported on December 30, 1857, that Lee's father-in-law had promised his slaves freedom in his will, and that the will was being kept secret. Lee angrily wrote the paper that the will was in probate and open for inspection. But he did not deny that the slaves who were now his had been promised their freedom. He kept them in slavery almost five more years, profiting from their free labor, before finally giving them their freedom in 1862.

While on leave at Arlington, Lee received an order from the War Department. In October 1859 abolitionist John Brown and nineteen armed men had captured the arsenal at Harpers Ferry, Virginia. Brown hoped that slaves throughout the state would join him in an uprising for freedom, but most Virginia slaves were too terrified to revolt, fearing they would be slaughtered.

Secretary of War John Floyd ordered Lee to take command of forces en route to Harpers Ferry. When Lee arrived there, he learned that Brown and his men had taken some hostages. Forbidding his troops to fire, Lee led a bayonet charge with a dozen men. One of Brown's followers raised a rifle to shoot Lee, but the shot went wild as a marine knocked the muzzle aside. The hostages were rescued, and Brown and his men were arrested.

Virginia hanged John Brown on December second, stirring a storm of protest among the nation's abolitionists. Eminent literary figures like Henry David Thoreau, Ralph Waldo Emerson, and Bronson Alcott held a "Martyr Service" to mourn him. Lee's only comment was, "The result proves that the plan was the attempt of a fanatic or a madman."

Southerners and some Northerners agreed. But millions of Northerners saw John Brown as a symbol of rebellion against the southern slave-owners' cruelties. Four years earlier this view of slavery had been dramatized by Harriet Beecher Stowe's popular novel, *Uncle Tom's Cabin*, which portrayed slaves as being worked brutally for plantation profits and whipped pitilessly when their owners were displeased.

When Lee rejoined his regiment in early 1860, he began to hear talk of secession over the slavery issue. Southerners were upset by the North's attempt to stop the spread of slavery to the territories. If slavery were stopped from expanding, many feared slaves in the southern states would grow restless and revolt, seeking the same freedom accorded blacks in the territories.

The debate intensified with the election of Abraham Lincoln in November. Although Lincoln was not an abolitionist, Southerners distrusted his Republican party, which was determined to keep slavery out of the territories.

Deeply troubled at the looming prospect of civil war, Lee told his Episcopalian bishop, J.F.B. Wilmer, "If the slaves of the South were mine, I would surrender them all without a struggle to avert this war." Despite this noble sentiment, he still refused his own slaves their freedom for another two years.

Lee was aware that secession by the South would put pressure on him either to remain in the Union army, or resign to join the Southern forces.

On New Year's Day 1861, when war seemed inevitable, Lee arrived at a decision. In a letter home he wrote, "Secession is nothing but revolution." He added, however, "If the Union is dissolved, and the Government disrupted, I shall return to my native State, and share the miseries of my people, and save in defense will draw my sword on none." It was clear that Lee's patriotism and loyalty were pledged, first and foremost, to his beloved state of Virginia.

On February 1, 1861, Texas seceded from the Union. Lee was ordered back to Washington. Arriving on March first, he was promoted to full colonel in command of the 1st Cavalry.

Then on April 12, 1861, South Carolina shore batteries fired on Fort Sumter in Charleston Harbor. The fort surrendered two days later to Lee's former comrade in the Mexican War, Pierre Beauregard, now a Confederate general.

Lee wondered gloomily whether the nation that his father and Washington had established in bloodshed was about to dissolve. On April sixteenth he heard that the Virginia convention had gone into secret session. The next day he received two messages. General Scott wanted Lee to call at his office in Washington. Francis P. Blair, Sr., a publicist close to Secretary of War Simon Cameron, also wanted urgently to see him.

Lee knew that his moment of decision had arrived: a decision that would change his whole life.

# 4

# Civilian Failure

Thirteen years earlier, in 1846, when Second Lieutenant Ulysses S. Grant found himself in the Mexican War, he marched to the Rio Grande with the army of General (later President) Zachary Taylor. He was without a horse because it had run away from the boy tending it. Rather than look for another one, he prepared to make the march on foot along with his men. But his captain insisted that a servant yield his horse to Grant.

The horse had never been saddled before. "For the first day there were frequent disagreements between us as to which way we should go," Grant wrote dryly, "and sometimes whether we should go at all."

On May third the Mexicans opened artillery fire, which was returned by American units. Miles away Grant began to have second thoughts about staying in the military. "As soon as this is over," he wrote Julia, "I will write to you again, that is, if I am one of the fortunate individuals who escape."

The war President Polk had sought to provoke had begun. Grant experienced his first baptism under fire at Palo Alto, where nine of his regiment were killed and forty-seven wounded.

"Although the balls were whizzing thick and fast about me," Grant wrote Julia, "I did not feel a sensation of fear until . . . a ball struck close by me killing one man instantly." But in the excitement of combat, he soon found his fear diminishing. After leading a charge at Resaca de la Palma, he told Julia, "There is no great sport in having bullets flying about one in every direction, but I find they have less horror when among them than in anticipation."

Grant was impressed by the lack of vanity of General Taylor, who rarely wore anything on his uniform to indicate his rank or even that he was an officer. "But he was known to every soldier in his army, and was respected by all," Grant noted.

When Taylor marched on Monterrey, Grant was left in charge of the regimental camp. Curiosity getting the better of him, he rode to the front to observe the battle. His pulse raced when he heard Taylor give the order to charge.

"Lacking the moral courage to return to camp — where I had been ordered to stay — I charged with the regiment," Grant reported. He rode with the army that entered Monterrey under fire. The general commanding the attack found his troops running out of ammunition. Grant volunteered to ride back through the heavy fighting to ask General Taylor for more ammunition and reinforcements.

"Before starting I adjusted myself on one side of

my horse furthest from the enemy," he related, "and with only one foot holding to the cantle of the saddle, and an arm over the neck of the horse exposed, I started at full run. It was only at street crossings that my horse was under fire, but these I crossed at such a flying rate that generally I was under cover of the next block of houses before the enemy fired."

His mission was successful. Monterrey fell.

"I thought how little interest the men before me had in the results of the war," he reflected, "and how little knowledge they had of 'what it was all about.' "

When General Scott was named supreme commander of the American forces in Mexico, Grant marched with him from Vera Cruz to the gates of Mexico City at San Cosme. Leading a small detachment of men and a short cannon called a howitzer, Grant took them through a hail of enemy fire to a church two hundred yards from the city. Pushing past a protesting priest, his men dragged the howitzer to the belfry, then bombarded the city's defenders.

His bold action proved so vital to forcing the entry into Mexico City that Grant was mentioned in dispatches to Washington. He was promoted to captain. Major Robert E. Lee interviewed him briefly, and mentioned Grant's feat in a report to General Scott.

\* \* \*

When Mexico City fell on September 14, 1847, the war was over. Grant became part of an army of occupation.

He felt compassion for the ragged, starving Mexicans.

"I pity poor Mexico," he wrote Julia. " . . . . The rich keep down the poor with a hardness of heart that is incredible."

Despite his sometimes gory battle experiences, Grant still maintained his horror of bloodshed. It was evident when he visited a Mexico City bullfight to view the national sport.

"The sight to me was sickening," he wrote. "I could not see how human beings could enjoy the sufferings of beasts, and often of men, as they seemed to do." He never went again.

Grant's experience in the Mexican War had let him test his courage in the heat of battle. It had taught him useful lessons in battlefield strategy. And it had allowed him to know and evaluate many military officers whom he would later serve with — and against — in the Civil War.

The American troops were withdrawn from Mexico in June 1848. Grant was sent to a camp in Mississippi. Obtaining leave, he returned to St. Louis and his beloved Julia. They were married on August twenty-second. Their marriage was to last thirty-seven years and produce four children. Julia Grant proved a devoted and fiercely loyal wife, despite all adversity, yet she never addressed him by his Christian name, always calling him "Mr. Grant."

Grant hoped that one of Julia's prosperous relatives would offer him a business connection. None did, perhaps realizing his lack of business sense. So he decided to stay in the army until something else turned up. During the next few years he was moved from one army post to another.

Transferred to the West Coast in 1852, he left Julia and their two children behind until he could afford to send for them. Missing them terribly, and bored by army life at the dreary frontier post of Fort Vancouver, the thirty-year-old Grant sought consolation for his loneliness in drinking.

"It was not that Grant drank much," a friend recalled. "The trouble was that a very little would . . . thicken his never glib or lively tongue. On far less liquor than many a comrade carried without a sign, Grant would appear half-stupefied." Grant's drinking was noted by General George B. McClellan.

Julia wrote her husband in 1853 urging him to be cautious about riding out alone lest Indians attack him. He replied, "Those Indians about here are the most harmless people you ever saw. It really is my opinion that the whole race would be harmless and peaceable if they were not put upon by the whites."

Trying to raise some extra money to send for his family, Grant invested all the salary he had earned on the West Coast in a San Francisco store, in a partnership with merchant Elijah Camp. He was persuaded to destroy Camp's I.O.U. for fifteen hundred dollars, after which Camp folded the business and sailed for New York.

That was the first of a long series of business disasters. Next Grant tried planting oats and potatoes as cash crops along the Columbia River. The river flooded, destroying the crops. He was transferred to Fort Humboldt in northern California under fussy Colonel James Buchanan, who disliked the sloppy junior officer.

"You do not know how forsaken I feel here," Grant wrote Julia. " . . . . I sometimes get so anxious to see you and our little boys, that I am almost tempted to resign and trust to Providence, and my own exertions, for a living where I can have you and them with me. . . . Whenever I get to thinking upon the subject, however, *poverty*, *poverty* begins to stare me in the face."

He tried again to supplement his income by running a billiard parlor as a sideline. This, too, failed.

Grant began to drink more heavily. In April 1854 he was discovered drunk by Colonel Buchanan. Ordering his arrest, Buchanan demanded that Grant either resign or stand trial for conduct unbecoming an officer. Grant submitted his resignation, to take effect on July 31.

When his anguished father learned about it, he

wrote Secretary of War Jefferson Davis to ask that his son's resignation — "the resignation of a war hero" — be rescinded.

But Davis, who had heard of Grant's reputation as an alcoholic, politely refused. Grant was once more a civilian.

"I was now to commence, at the age of thirty-two, a new struggle for our support," he wrote later. Julia's father gave them a farm near St. Louis. Grant cleared the land, squared logs, built a house for them, and hauled cordwood for sale.

He was forced to stop working on the farm when he fell ill with undiagnosed chills, fever, and coughing fits. In the fall of 1858 he had to sell his stock, crops, and equipment at auction. Grant gave up farming. Another failure.

Things grew so desperate for him that he had to pawn his gold watch for twenty-two dollars to buy Christmas presents for Julia and the children. He no longer even owned a horse.

Ever loyal, Julia fiercely defended her husband against all criticism. "I have been both indignant and grieved," she fumed, "over the statements of pretended personal acquaintances of Captain Grant at this time to the effect that he was dejected, low-spirited, badly dressed, and even slovenly. Well, I am quite sure they did not know *my* Captain Grant, for he was always perfection."

At age thirty-seven, Grant had to swallow his pride — what was left of it — and ask his father for a job in his leather goods business in Galena, Illinois, an outgrowth of the tannery.

His father made him a clerk at eight hundred dollars a year, with the humiliation of having to work under his two younger brothers. He proved an incompetent clerk, seldom able to remember the price of any merchandise. In fact, his mind was elsewhere.

Although his experience in battle had intensified his distaste for bloodshed, it had also increased his interest in military strategy. Sitting in the leather store, he read newspapers and studied maps to follow the campaign of Napoleon III in Italy in 1859. He would comment on attacks he considered mistaken, and announce what his strategy would have been instead.

Otherwise life was bleak and disappointing for the army hero who had become a civilian failure. One friend privately referred to Grant as a "broken man," a far cry from the dashing young captain on the Mexican battlefield.

When the Civil War broke out, Grant was still clerking in his brothers' leather store. He did not, at first, think of volunteering. He was convinced, like Lincoln's secretary of state, William H. Seward, that "the war will be over in ninety days." But when Grant realized that it wouldn't be, he contemplated returning to uniform to serve his country once again.

Provided the U.S. army, which had forced him out for drunkenness, was willing to have him back.

## 5

# "Through Mud, Snow and Rain"

When President-Elect Abraham Lincoln left for his inauguration in Washington, threats of assassination made it necessary to whisk him off his train from Springfield, Illinois. He was smuggled into the capital through Baltimore.

Grant, Lee, and Lincoln all knew that when the American flag was hauled down at Fort Sumter by the Confederates, this insult and challenge to the Stars and Stripes made civil war inevitable. Emotions that had been running high between North and South now grew frenzied.

On April 15, 1861, Lincoln declared the existence of an "insurrection." He called for 75,000 Northern volunteers to give three months of military service to put it down. By that time seven Southern states, but not Virginia, had joined South Carolina in breaking away from the Union. Two days later Lincoln proclaimed a Union blockade of the entire southern coast.

So began the only war in which American citizens have ever fought against Americans. This hadn't been the case in 1776 because the war then had pitted anti-British colonists against British loyalists and Britons.

Lee, unlike Grant, was convinced that the conflict would be a long one. He believed that Lincoln and his generals seriously underestimated what it would take to crush the revolt.

Although Lee didn't know it, a Virginia Secession Convention had met in secret on April 17, voting to join the seceding states. The following day Lee met with politician Francis Blair at his home across from the White House. Blair, speaking for Lincoln, offered Lee command of the Northern army being raised to fight the Confederacy. Lee shook his head.

"I oppose secession and I deprecate war," he said, "yet I can take no part in an invasion of the Southern states."

Leaving Blair, Lee went to see General Scott, who also urged him to accept the command. Lee regretfully declined.

"The property belonging to my children, and all they possess, lies in Virginia," he explained. "They will be ruined, if they do not go with their state. I cannot raise my hand against my children."

"You're making the greatest mistake of your life," Scott told Lee sadly. "I suggest that if you intend to resign from the army, you should do so promptly."

Deeply disturbed, Lee felt torn between allegiance to the American flag he had served so long and so well, and loyalty to his native Virginia. He did not support slavery, but he did support the right of each state to secede if it wished, because Lee believed the Declaration of Independence gave each state the right to retain its sovereignty.

Abolition was not the real issue that divided North and South originally. The North fought primarily for the preservation of the Union. The Southern states fought for the right to secede from a government they did not support because they felt it threatened their slave economy.

While paying a bill in a drugstore, Lee learned that Virginia had joined the secession. He was upset by this development, but now felt that he had no choice but to send his resignation from the U.S. army to Secretary of War Simon Cameron.

"I have not been able to make up my mind to raise my hand against my relatives, my children, my home," he wrote a sister. "I have therefore resigned my commission in the army, and, save in defense of my native state — with the sincere hope that my poor service may never be needed — I hope I may never be called upon to draw my sword."

It was anything but easy for Lee to separate himself from the service to which he had given thirty-six years of his life. The decision not only cost him his Union Army career, but also separated him from friends and relatives who chose the Union side.

Lee had no illusions that the South, with a population of only nine million, could easily defend itself against the North's population of twenty-two million. Aware that the industrializing North also had far more resources with which to wage war than the still primarily agricultural South, he was filled with foreboding.

When Lincoln's call for army volunteers reached Galena, Illinois, a public meeting was called. Grant was chosen to preside because of having been a West Pointer and captain in the Mexican War. A local company was raised, and Grant was offered its captaincy. Still wary of the military life, he declined, but promised to aid the new company any way he could.

But this new recognition seemed to have a restorative effect on the civilian failure. "I saw new energies in Grant," his neighborhood friend John Rawlins declared, adding, "He dropped a stoop-shouldered way of walking, and set his hat forward on his forehead in a careless fashion."

Grant himself acknowledged the change that came over him. "I never once went into our leather store after that meeting," he said, "to put up a package or do other business."

Organizing enlisted men for the company, he went off with them in civilian clothes to Camp Yates in Springfield. Once again he refused the post of captain, because now he hoped to be recalled by the regular army with the rank and pay of colonel.

In the first few weeks of the war, there was almost a carnival atmosphere in both the North and South. Patriotic parades took to the streets with bands playing and flags flying, inspiring enlistments. So many Southerners and Northerners sought to join their armies that both governments lacked enough uniforms, weapons, and equipment for them, nor had enough cooks to feed them.

This enthusiasm for the war came before the first blood had been shed. Later both sides had trouble conscripting troops.

Meanwhile in Virginia, Lee's friend, Governor John Letcher, summoned him to Richmond, which had been named the capital of the new Confederacy. When Lee arrived there on April 22, 1861, Letcher offered him command of the military and naval forces of Virginia, with the rank of major general.

Lee accepted this command to protect Virginia from a Northern invasion. He was aware that Arlington's commanding site high on a bluff overlooking the capital made it a prime target for Federal troops. Lee wondered sadly if he would ever be able to return to the house he had known since childhood.

His first act as a general was to send Colonel Thomas Jackson, soon to be known as Stonewall Jackson, to seize Harpers Ferry from Federal forces.

On April 24 Virginia entered into a military alliance with the Confederacy. Now, Lee would fight for the Confederacy as well as Virginia.

This was made clear to him on May 15 by Confederate President Jefferson Davis. He appointed Lee brigadier general in the regular army of the Confederacy. Technically this put Lee in command of all Southern forces. But only three weeks later Davis appointed himself commander-in-chief, with Lee becoming his unofficial chief of staff.

Although Davis greatly admired Lee, he preferred himself, not Lee or any of the other Southern generals, to be considered the central figure of the South's struggle for independence. However, Lee handled Davis with such tact that Davis generally approved Lee's battle plans.

Lee would ask Davis to visit him in the field, writing, "I need not say how glad I should be if your convenience would permit you to visit the army, that I might have the benefit of your advice and direction," which Lee then would skillfully maneuver around to whatever he wanted to do. Other generals saw such deferential treatment of Davis as bootlicking. Lee admitted his displeasure with the arrangement by writing Mary that he could see neither "advantage or pleasure" in his new assignment, but was resigned to it as his duty.

In this respect Lee differed from Grant. When Grant eventually achieved command of the Union forces, he often disregarded orders from the U.S. War Department. He ran the war as he saw fit, often infuriating the Union army high command.

Lee felt that he had a military tradition to live up to — the reputation of his boyhood idol Washington and of his father, Light-Horse Harry Lee. He now saw himself as their shieldbearer, defending their Virginia with "my sword, and, if need be, with my life." This resolution stiffened when Federal troops invaded northeast Virginia on May 27, seizing Arlington, and making the house of Robert E. Lee a military headquarters of the U.S. army.

On that same day Grant, still a civilian, wrote to the adjutant-general of the U.S. army to request command of a regiment "if the President, in his judgment, should see fit to intrust one to me." He received no answer.

He asked to see George B. McClellan, with whom Grant had served in the Mexican War, and who was now a major general, soon to command all the Union armies. McClellan refused to see him, aware of Grant's expulsion from the army for alcoholism.

Even as Grant asked for a regiment, he admitted to a friend, "To tell you the truth . . . there are few men really competent to command a thousand soldiers, and I doubt whether I am one of them."

So he was greatly surprised when Illinois Governor Richard Yates offered to recommend Grant for the rank of brigadier general. Grant felt so awed by the suggestion that he replied, "I don't want such office until I've earned it."

Baffled, Yates asked a bookkeeper from the Galena leather store, "What *does* Grant want?" The bookkeeper replied, "The way to deal with him is to ask him no questions, but simply *order* him to duty. He'll obey promptly."

So that was what Yates did. He sent an order to Grant: "You are this day appointed colonel of the 21st Illinois Volunteers, and requested to take command at once."

On June 15 Grant left for their camp on fairgrounds near Springfield. He arrived there with General John E. Smith.

"I went with him to camp," Smith recalled, "and shall never forget the scene when his men first saw him. Grant was dressed in citizen's clothes, an old coat worn out at the elbows, and a badly damaged hat. His men, though ragged and barefooted themselves, had formed a high estimate of what a colonel should be, and when Grant walked in among them, they began making fun of him. They cried in derision, 'What a colonel!' 'Damn such a colonel!'. . . . And one of them, to show off to the others, got behind his back and commenced sparring at him, and while he was doing this another gave him such a push that he hit Grant between the shoulders."

"They're an unruly lot," one of Governor Yates's

aides said nervously to Grant. "Do you think you can manage them?"

"Oh, yes," Grant replied. He recognized that he would not be dealing with professional soldiers, as in the Mexican War. The men mockingly called out for a speech.

Grant's speech consisted of five words.

"Men, go to your quarters!" he snapped.

Not having been at a battalion drill for fifteen years, during which time military tactics had changed, Grant found it necessary to study a drill lesson each night. Teaching it to his officers, he then had the regiment perform it next day.

"I do not believe," he wrote, "that the officers of the regiment ever discovered that I had never studied the tactics that I used."

Grant was ordered to lead his regiment into Missouri to forestall Confederates trying to take over that state. On the march he found every house in his path deserted.

Approaching the brow of a hill, he could see the enemy camp of Confederate Colonel Thomas Harris. He worried that the rebels were dug in, waiting to open fire.

"My heart kept getting higher and higher," he admitted, "until it felt to me as though it was in my throat. I would have given anything then to have been back in Illinois, but I had not the moral courage to halt and consider what to do; I kept right on." As always, Grant refused to turn aside from an objective he was determined to reach, however threatening.

To his immense relief he found the Confederate campsite totally deserted. "My heart resumed its place," he sighed. "It occurred to me at once that Harris had been as much afraid of me as I had been of him. This was a view of the question I had never taken before; but it was one I never forgot afterwards. From that event to the close of the war, I never experienced trepidation upon confronting an enemy. . . . I never forgot that he had as much reason to fear my forces as I had his. The lesson was valuable."

Because the South needed to raise manpower for their army much sooner than the more heavily populated North, the Confederacy passed a conscription act early in 1862 (which Lee supported), a year before the Northern conscription act. Draftees in the Confederate army were not happy about an exemption for owners of fifteen or more slaves. The reason given was that the large plantation owners were needed to produce the cotton the South sold abroad, and to grow food for the Confederate army.

To make Southern conscription more acceptable, Lee decreed that conscriptees could elect their own field and company officers. They even had the right to decide in the trenches which officers should lead them into battle, and often did so. These concessions helped hold down grumbling by draftees, and made the Confederate army more democratic, but also less disciplined.

Life in the trenches of Virginia was described by a private in the summer of 1861: "Short rations, thin and ragged clothing, rain, mud, water and measles, all mixed together."

Lee blocked the Union line of advance by entrenching Confederate troops under Brigadier General Pierre Beauregard south of the stream called Bull Run, near Manassas, Virginia. General Scott, now commanding the Union forces, sent Brigadier General Irvin McDowell's army to attack Beauregard.

The battle was fought on a Sunday, so that many Washingtonians were free from work and were picnicking on the battlefield, only thirty miles from the capital. Civilians in those days knew nothing about a battle, so they regarded it much as spectators might think of a boxing match. They jammed the roads in buggies to watch the fighting, enjoying the booming of cannon, the battlefield smoke, and the spectacle of distant soldiers running at and away from each other.

The Battle of Bull Run, or Manassas, began on July 21, a hot, sunny day. To the dismay of Northerners, Thomas J. Jackson, now a general, withstood the brunt of the Union attack, then led a roaring counterattack that routed McDowell's army. Panicked Federals dropped their guns and fled.

Now the frightened spectators began jamming the roads and bridges back to Washington. Their carriages tried to get through at the same time as army wagons and cannons, causing a traffic grid-lock that worsened when a bridge broke down. Both soldiers and civilians were terrified that they would be slain by Jackson's pursuing forces.

Fortunately for them, the Confederates were so confused by their unexpected victory that they failed to pursue the fleeing soldiers in blue and wipe out McDowell's army.

During the battle, when a Confederate officer was trying to rally his men against the Union at-tack, he cried, "Look — there's Jackson standing like a stone wall! Rally behind the Virginians!" From then on the Confederate hero of Bull Run became known as Stonewall Jackson.

Lee was irked because Jefferson Davis had kept him at Confederate headquarters in Richmond dur-ing the battle. "I wished to partake in the . . . struggle," he wrote Mary in disappointment, "and am mortified at my absence."

Northerners were shocked and dismayed by the defeat of the inexperienced Union army at Bull Run, the first clash of the Civil War. It shook the belief of many that the war would be short, with an early Union victory. Southerners were delighted by the outcome of Bull Run, which gave them an exaggerated idea of the fighting abilities of their soldiers. It led them to underestimate the troops of the North. Many saw the battle as the forerunner of an early Confederate victory.

Two weeks after Bull Run, Grant read in a paper that Lincoln had asked Illinois congressmen to recommend some Illinois citizens for the rank of brigadier general. To Grant's surprise, they had unanimously recommended him as first on a list of seven. On August 7 he received his new commission, and was placed in charge of Federal troops in southern Illinois and southeast Missouri.

He at once summoned his friend, young hometown lawyer John A. Rawlins, to become his assistant adjutant-general with the rank of captain. Rawlins gave up an appointment as major of a new regiment to join Grant, and became his trusted confidante throughout the war. When Grant gave in to his weakness for alcohol, only Rawlins could persuade him to stop.

Grant moved swiftly when he learned that a Confederate force was heading to capture Paducah, Kentucky, at the mouth of the Tennessee River. Kentucky was then officially neutral in the war, out of fear of the Union army. On September 6, 1861, Grant put his troops and artillery on steamboats, and led them with gunboats, beating the Confederates to Paducah.

He told Kentuckians, "I have come among you, not as an enemy, but as your friend and fellow citizen. . . . An enemy, in rebellion against our common government . . . is moving upon your city. I am here to defend you." Having reached the Tennessee River, his forces became known as the Army of the Tennessee.

Grant's first Civil War battle occurred on November 7 when he received orders to attack Belmont, Missouri. He led 3,100 men against 2,500 Confederates. At first his charges swept the rebel army aside and routed it. His troops cheered jubilantly at their first battle victory.

But suddenly Confederate reinforcements attacked Grant's flanks. His army was surrounded and cut off from their river transports. Grant's officers panicked, telling him there was now no option but surrender.

"Nonsense!" Grant snapped. "We cut our way in, and we can cut our way out." He directed action to sweep aside the Confederates who were blocking their escape. His men raced for their boats. As Grant ordered the wounded carried aboard, his horse was shot out from under him. He merely sprang aboard the horse of a cavalryman who had been shot.

Confederate General Leonidas Polk wired Jefferson Davis jubilantly, "General Grant is reported killed."

By this time all Grant's remaining troops were

aboard their transports. The boats began pulling away from shore rapidly as pursuing enemy troops opened fire upon them. Grant was the only Union army man left between the rebels and the departing transports. The captain of one transport, spotting Grant, yelled an order to stop the engine. A fifteen-foot plank was hastily put out from the ship to the riverbank.

Grant slid his horse down the bank, and trotted him aboard the boat over a single gangplank.

Resting momentarily on a sofa below deck, he rose to watch the rebels firing on the transports. A musket ball struck the sofa where his head had been just seconds before.

Subsequently a truce was arranged aboard a Confederate boat to allow both sides to bury their dead. Ironically, the atmosphere of the truce boat was friendly, with lunch served by the Confederates, as though after a sports event.

Despite his rout, Grant called the Battle of Belmont a Union victory, since his forces had captured 175 prisoners and 2 big guns. But his casualties were 600 men, with the Confederates losing an equal number.

"It is called a victory," one Union officer wrote bitterly, "but if such be victory, God save us from defeat!"

That fall General Scott was relieved as Commanding General of the Union armies by General

McClellan. Placed in personal command of the Army of the Potomac, McClellan was expected both to defend Washington and attack Richmond.

The change that affected Grant directly, however, was the replacement of General John C. Fremont as commander of the department of Missouri by General Henry Wagner Halleck. Halleck was a jealous, vindictive man who disliked Grant intensely because of Grant's tendency to take action on his own, without waiting for permission from higher authority.

After the Battle of Belmont, Halleck kept Grant's troops idle for three months until early February 1862. They grew restless and bored, especially by meals consisting largely of salt pork or bacon and hardtack, a tough soda cracker. To make coffee they had to grind the beans in a bucket with the butt of a musket.

Meanwhile Grant had time to think about the larger issues of the war. "My inclination," he wrote Julia, "is to whip the rebellion into submission, preserving all constitutional rights. . . . If it is necessary that slavery should fall that the Republic may continue its existence, let slavery go."

But he didn't think the time was right for that yet. Neither did Lincoln, who feared losing the border states to the South if he were to free the slaves.

However, Grant strongly disapproved of the Federal Fugitive Slave Law, requiring the return of runaway slaves to their masters. Acting on his own, he issued an order preventing the operation of the act in the territory he controlled.

Restless at being kept out of action, Grant tried to get Halleck to approve a new military campaign he had planned to capture Fort Henry and Fort Donelson at the Tennessee border.

But Halleck, hearing fresh rumors about Grant's drinking, refused his request. Instead Halleck ordered him to take his troops on reconnaissance maneuvers, which Grant considered pointless in the middle of a war.

They amounted to no more, he wrote in disgust, than "splashing through the mud, snow and rain."

That was hardly the way to win the war.

# 6

# Fighting Generals

Lee was also restless under the restraints that Jefferson Davis placed upon him. He hoped for a field command instead of being confined to Richmond under Davis's thumb.

"I do not know what my position will be," he wrote Mary on June 9, 1861. "I should like to retire to private life, so that I could be with you and the children, but if I can be of service to the State or her cause, I must continue."

As a military strategist he made a mistake in getting Davis to agree to divide a force of poorly trained, poorly armed troops in western Virginia to stop an attack by McClellan. McClellan was able to overwhelm them in less than three months after secession.

Now Davis did send Lee into the field to reverse the situation. Lee found himself with a hornet's nest on his hands. The two Confederate generals who had failed to stop McClellan were feuding, blaming each other. Lee failed to use his authority to force them to cooperate. The result was a collapse of the effort to save western Virginia, which fell to McClellan.

Removing Lee from the Virginia command,

Davis put him instead in charge of coastal defenses of South Carolina, Georgia, and Florida. Their ports were essential to the Confederacy for the South's exports and imports.

Using his expertise as an army engineer, and his successful experience in the Mexican War, Lee strengthened the defenses of the coastal forts during the first half of 1862. He rode along his lines daily, making suggestions to working parties and encouraging their efforts.

Lee's basic battle strategy was based on his belief that well-entrenched soldiers with artillery could be counted on to beat off three times their number of attackers. It was a strategy later used in twentieth-century wars. But Southern papers criticized Lee for "digging in" instead of taking the offensive.

"I am sorry . . . that the movements of the armies cannot keep pace with the expectations of the editors of the papers," Lee wrote Mary sarcastically.

He sought to establish high morale among his troops by eliminating officer privileges. He made his headquarters in the field simply a group of pole-tents. His staff was crowded together, two or three to a tent. Eating the same food as privates, Lee sent food gifts given him to the sick and wounded.

If his manner was somewhat austere, his men found him a perfect Southern gentleman — kind, generous, and modest. Almost always polite, on the rare occasions he lost his temper and bawled

*A portrait of Ulysses S. Grant taken by the famous
photographer Mathew Brady.*

*Julia Dent Grant,
Grant's wife.*

*Jesse and Hannah Grant, the parents of Ulysses S. Grant.*

*Abraham Lincoln.*

*The charge of Grant at the Battle of Shiloh.*

*General William Tecumseh Sherman.*

*The infamous Andersonville prison.*

*Grant with his staff in 1864.*

*Grant's reception after Lee's surrender.*

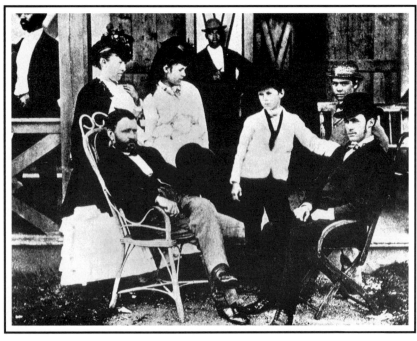

*Grant with his family and servants.*

*Ulysses S. Grant, President from 1869-1877.*

Copyrighted July 22d 85

*Grant a few days before he died.*

a man out, he was quick to make amends if he learned that he had been wrong.

That happened once after he had scolded a scout. Informed he had been unfair to the man, Lee had his orderly prepare a supper with hot coffee for the scout, seat him in Lee's camp chair, and serve the meal at Lee's table.

To Lee, being unfair to any of his men was unthinkable, even in the heat of battle. He played no favorites, and tried to give every man the merit he deserved.

Lee was also available to any soldier with a problem or complaint. It was not surprising that, more than any general on either side of the war, Lee inspired great loyalty, devotion, and respect from his soldiers. Many fought more for Lee than for the Confederate cause. One of his staff, Colonel Charles Marshall, declared, ''To them he represented cause, country, and all.''

When Joe Johnston was wounded in battle near Richmond, Lee was sent to replace him. In June McClellan attacked Lee's forces near Mechanicsville, Virginia, with an artillery barrage. Jefferson Davis arrived at the front to find Lee standing in an exposed position.

''Why, General,'' he exclaimed, ''what are you doing here? You are in too dangerous a position for command of the army.''

''I am trying to find out something about the

movements and plans of those people," Lee replied. "But you must excuse me, Mr. President, for asking what *you* are doing here."

"I am on the same mission that you are."

Confederate General A.P. Hill rode up to them and snapped, "This is no place for *either* of you, and as commander of this part of the field, I order you both to the rear!"

They backed up a few yards as the shells flew even thicker. Hill galloped up again angrily.

"Didn't I tell you to go away from here? . . . . Why, one shell from that battery over yonder may deprive the Confederacy of its President and the army of its commander!"

Lee and Davis retreated meekly.

Grant, like Lee, inspired the respect of his men, but he seemed more remote to them. He was so shy that before taking a bath, he would close the flaps of his tent carefully so that no one could see him naked. His officers thought nothing of standing in the open as orderlies poured water over them.

General Halleck continued to ignore Grant's persistent requests for permission to attack Forts Henry and Donelson, both in Tennessee, until Navy Flag Officer Andrew Hull Foote supported the plan in January 1862. Then Halleck reluctantly agreed to a joint army-navy expedition.

Navy gunboats and Grant's 17,000 troops on transports attacked Fort Henry on the Tennessee

River on February 6. To test the range of enemy fire, Grant boarded a gunboat and requested its captain to approach the fort until fired upon. One shot passed close to where they were standing. Knowing now the range of the enemy's fire power, Grant's troops disembarked safely beyond it.

The Confederate commander of Fort Henry fought a delaying battle to give the bulk of his troops time to escape to Fort Donelson before surrendering Fort Henry along with ninety men.

McClellan, who had never held too high an opinion of Grant, was now so pleased that he told Halleck, "Please thank Grant and Foote and their commands for me."

But Halleck congratulated Foote only, ignoring Grant.

On February 11 Grant and Foote advanced on Fort Donelson on the Cumberland River. Grant surrounded it on land while Foote's gunboats attacked from the river. A Confederate force of 5,300 men attacked the Federals and drove them back.

Returning from a conference with Foote, Grant found his men reeling in confusion. A staff officer, white with fear, shouted, "We are cut to pieces!"

Unruffled, Grant told his staff coolly, "Gentlemen, the position must be retaken." Galloping down the line, he called, "Fill your cartridge boxes quick and get into line. The enemy is trying to escape, and he must not be permitted to!"

Later he said, "This acted like a charm. The men

only wanted someone to give them a command."
Grant's presence in the face of danger revitalized
the Federals and restored their confidence. He
watched in satisfaction as they fought back so
fiercely that Confederate General Simon B. Buckner felt compelled to ask for an armistice to discuss
terms of surrender.

"No terms except unconditional and immediate
surrender can be accepted," Grant replied firmly.
"I propose to move immediately upon your
works."

Buckner, who had befriended Grant at West
Point and had served with him in Mexico, replied
sourly, "The overwhelming force under your command compels me . . . to accept the ungenerous
and unchivalrous terms which you propose."

Grant took over Fort Donelson, capturing a
whole Confederate army. He reported to Halleck
that he had seized up to 15,000 prisoners, 4,000
horses, and huge stacks of arms. Refusing to return
to their masters slaves who had worked at the fort,
Grant later offered instead to let them join the
Union army.

The capture of Fort Donelson was the first important Union victory in the Civil War. It created
a storm of excitement in the North. Northerners
recognized it as the most damaging blow inflicted
on the South up to that time, winning Kentucky
and opening all of Tennessee to Federal invasion.

Grant became an instant military hero. The media exulted that his initials "U.S." stood for "Unconditional Surrender." Secretary of War Edwin P. Stanton asserted jubilantly that the aggressive spirit that would win the war was perfectly expressed in Grant's ultimatum to Buckner.

When a newspaper correspondent described Grant as smoking a cigar while directing the battle, enthusiastic Northerners deluged him with boxes of cigars. Poverty having taught Grant frugality, he gave up pipe-smoking for cigars.

Lincoln promoted him to major general of volunteers, making Grant outrank every general in the West except Halleck.

The defeat at Fort Donelson depressed Lee and Jefferson Davis. Southerners in Nashville, the capital of Tennessee, fell into a blind panic because they were now open to attack from Donelson. Nashville had never been fortified, and its citizens knew it was a prime target as an important supply base and industrial center. Frightened citizens braced for its fall.

On February 21 Grant and Foote set an expeditionary force afloat with just that goal. They were stunned when Halleck telegraphed Grant that the gunboats were not to proceed.

One reason was Halleck's resentment of Grant's sudden popularity and promotion, fearing him as a rival for high command. Halleck aspired to senior command of the whole war in the West on the strength of the Donelson victory. To reduce Grant's stature, he asked McClellan to make two other generals, Don Carlos Buell and John Pope, major generals equal with Grant. And Halleck asked that he himself be made commander-in-chief above all three.

But Halleck reckoned without Abraham Lincoln. The president, admiring Grant's fighting ability, sent to the Senate only his recommendation for Grant's promotion. Halleck was furious. Grant managed to lose communication with him as he drove eastward through Tennessee. Halleck chose to view his failure to communicate as an act of insubordination.

"I have no communication with General Grant for more than a week," he complained to McClellan. "He left his command without my authority and went to Nashville. . . . It is hard to censure a successful general immediately after a victory, but I think he richly deserves it."

McClellan, still no admirer of Grant, replied, "Generals must observe discipline as well as private soldiers. Do not hesitate to arrest him at once if the good of the service requires it."

Halleck added fuel to the fire by wiring McClellan that rumor had it Grant had "resumed his former bad habits," referring to Grant's drinking problem. He then wired Grant an order to remain at Fort Henry. And he demanded, "Why do you not obey my orders to report strength and positions of your command?"

Grant simply denied that he had received earlier messages from Halleck. And he coldly requested to be relieved from further duty under his hostile commander. At this point Lincoln entered the picture, ordering a full report of the conflict between them. Fearing exposure of his jealous spite, Halleck hastily backed down. He assured Lincoln that "irregularities have now been remedied."

He wrote Grant, "Instead of relieving you, I wish you, as soon as your new army is in the field, to assume immediate command, and lead it to new victories."

Early in March McClellan was relieved as commander-in-chief to concentrate on an Army of the Potomac campaign against Richmond. Halleck was placed in command of all the Federal forces in the West. Grant reassumed his command on March 17 at Savannah, Tennessee. He was anxious to attack Corinth, Mississippi, before the Confederates could strengthen defenses there, but Halleck ordered him to wait until his army was reinforced by the Army of the Ohio led by General Buell.

Hearing shooting on the night of April 4, Grant rode to the front in a pouring rain to investigate. His horse slipped and fell on Grant's leg. For several days Grant had to hobble painfully on crutches.

Meanwhile 45,000 Confederates had massed just two miles from General Tecumseh Sherman's unsuspecting Union encampment at Shiloh, Tennessee. The first major clash between forces controlled by Grant and Lee was about to take place.

On March 13, 1862, Lee was made commander-in-chief of the Confederate army under Jefferson Davis. He was charged specifically with the defense of the Confederate capital, Richmond.

Lee had hoped, along with Davis, that Britain might interfere in the war on the side of the Confederacy to protect its trade with the South. But now he dismissed that hope, writing, "We must make up our minds to fight our battles ourselves. Expect to receive aid from no one."

Lee was determined to strike at Grant's army quickly. He wrote General Albert Johnston at Corinth, "I need you, when your army is united, to deal a blow at the enemy in your front, if possible before his rear gets up from Nashville. You have him divided; keep him so if you can."

Johnston promptly joined his forces to those of Generals Beauregard and Braxton Bragg. On April 6 he led a surprise attack on Sherman's forces at Shiloh, seeking to drive them into the Tennessee River. Many of the Union troops were raw recruits. Whole regiments panicked and fled. Sherman had two horses shot out from under him, and was wounded in the hand.

The Union forces at Shiloh were almost annihilated on the first day of battle. Grant quickly boarded a river ship, hobbling off on his crutches at Pittsburg Landing in southwest Tennessee. Here at the front he had to be helped onto his horse, the crutches strapped to his saddle. Riding for a rendezvous with Sherman, he was suddenly confronted by the spectacle of 5,000 frantic Union soldiers fleeing from the battlefield at Shiloh under a barrage of heavy artillery fire.

Grant galloped through the terrified troops. Rallying them, he turned them around to face the enemy and rode to the front with them. By fighting from morning to night, he was able to hold off the enemy until Buell's forces finally arrived to join the battle.

At night, drenched in a fierce rainstorm, Grant made his headquarters under a tree. His leg was now so badly swollen that he could get no rest. After midnight, severe pain drove him to a loghouse used as a hospital.

"All night wounded men were being brought in, their wounds dressed, a leg or an arm amputated as the case might require," he wrote, "and everything being done to save life or alleviate suffering. The sight was more unendurable than encountering the enemy's fire, and I returned to my tree in the rain."

At heart Grant was really a pacifist appalled by the bloodshed of war. "I never liked service in the army," he admitted years later. What appealed to him on the battlefield was the challenge of pitting his strategy against obstacles and overcoming them, outwitting his opponent — the same enjoyment he found in chess.

On the second day of the battle at Shiloh Confederates attacked unexpectedly from Grant's right flank. "The shells and balls whistled about our ears very fast for about a minute," he recorded. "I do not think it took us longer than that to get out of range and out of sight." One shot struck the metal scabbard of Grant's sword, breaking it off.

Instead of retreating before the new Confederate attack, Grant decided on a daring counterattack. Rallying his men, he cried, "Advance and recapture our original camp!" He led a fierce charge that forced the Confederates to fall back. In the bloody fighting General Johnston was wounded and bled to death.

Beauregard assumed command of the Confederate forces. He led a retreat to Corinth, leaving behind a battleground strewn with rebel and Union bodies. Grant refused to order a pursuit of Beauregard, for which he was later severely criticized.

"I wanted to pursue," he explained, "but had not the heart to order the men who had fought desperately for two days . . . to pursue."

The Battle of Shiloh, which came to be known as "Bloody Shiloh," cost each side more than 10,000 casualties. That was 500 more than had fallen in the American Revolution, War of 1812, and Mexican War combined.

Lee was chagrined at the Confederates' failure to send the Union army reeling back at Shiloh. Had they won, they would have reversed all the Union successes in the Tennessee Valley. Their failure to win had laid the South open to a Union drive into the heart of the Confederacy.

Lee was also saddened by reports from Corinth of 16,000 Confederate soldiers wounded, many facing amputation of limbs. Short of drugs to combat tetanus and gangrene, hard-pressed Confederate doctors estimated that eighty percent of the soldiers whose limbs they had to amputate would die.

For Grant, Shiloh represented a hollow victory, because both sides still held exactly the same positions as before the battle. The fierce fighting of the Southern forces at Shiloh convinced Grant that the North's optimistic expectations of an early collapse of the Confederate armies were unrealistic. He also realized that the whole South, not just the South's men under arms, would need to be defeated for a total victory.

"I gave up all idea of saving the Union except by complete conquest," he declared later.

He forgave the Union troops, young men only recently from farms and towns, who had panicked at their first encounter with deadly enemy fire. Later he insisted that "better troops never went on a battlefield." But he was outraged at the colonels, majors, and captains who had also fled at Shiloh, leaving their men leaderless as they ran to save their own skins.

Grant learned from the tactical mistakes he had made at Shiloh, such as placing his forces with their backs to a river. He did not repeat them again, unlike Lee, who repeated his mistakes in the western Virginia campaign on the second day of the Battle of Gettysburg.

The Northern press again applauded Grant as a war hero and hailed the Battle of Shiloh as a great victory, raising Northern spirits. But Grant could only think sadly of the horrible sight of thousands of bloody bodies strewn over the battlefield like so many rag dolls.

Not all the Northern media shared the enthusiasm for Grant. Some papers raised the old issue of his drinking, charging that his men lacked respect for him for that reason. They cited reports that after a battle he would disappear to get drunk, and had to be protected by his staff. Battlefield pictures of Grant in his shabby, rumpled uniform supported the charges.

One editorial called him a "a disgraceful figure of a general," and demanded his removal. But Lincoln was firm in his faith in Grant as a "can-do" general who could and would accomplish any mission given him.

"I can't spare this man," Lincoln would reply to Grant's critics. "He fights." To a temperance committee protesting Grant's drinking, Lincoln replied dryly, "I'd like to know where General Grant gets his whisky so that I can send a barrel to some of our other generals!"

At the same time the president was appalled at the casualties at Shiloh. General John McClernand, envious of Grant and eager to take his place, reported to Lincoln that the Union losses in the battle had been a "slaughter." Disturbed, Lincoln told Secretary of War Stanton to wire Halleck asking whether the heavy losses could reflect Grant's negligence.

The hostile Halleck's reply suggested that Grant's alcoholism was indeed a problem. Stanton gave Halleck permission to transfer command of Grant's Army of the Tennessee to General George H. Thomas. Halleck also took field command of the Armies of the West himself. He downgraded Grant to the post of second in command, then totally ignored him.

Outraged, Grant wanted to resign from the army, but was persuaded not to by his friend General Sherman, who had joined Grant's command just before the Battle of Shiloh.

When Halleck's forces marched on Corinth, Mississippi, the Confederate armies abandoned the city. Halleck boasted to Lincoln that he had won a great victory.

But early in June 1862 Halleck simply barricaded his troops at Corinth behind extensive earthworks instead of driving on to attack Fredericksburg. Disgusted, Grant realized that Halleck had given Lee valuable time to reinforce the rebel army.

On June 1 Lee was given command of the armies in eastern Virginia and northern Carolina. To thwart the Union drive southward, he ordered his generals to pretend an attack on Washington and cause Union forces to be recalled to defend the capital. Lee's ruse worked.

McClellan had begun a push toward Richmond. But Lincoln and Stanton, frightened by Lee's bluff, compelled McClellan to detach 50,000 of his troops near Washington to protect it. McClellan blamed this for his failure to take Richmond in the spring of 1862.

Memphis, Tennessee, fell to Union forces by June 6, 1862. Federal control of the Mississippi River now extended as far south as the vicinity of Vicksburg. Grant asked Halleck to be allowed to remove his headquarters to Memphis. His request approved, he started there with his staff and a cavalry escort.

On the way he spent the night at the house of a man loyal to the Union. Later he learned that Stonewall Jackson's forces passed where he had been on the road less than an hour later.

"Had Jackson gone three-quarters of a mile farther," Grant wrote, "he would have found me with my party quietly resting under the shade of trees and without even arms in our hands with which to defend ourselves."

When Jackson later found this out, he expressed chagrin at having missed the opportunity to capture Grant.

When McClellan's main Union army speared toward Richmond, Lee developed a daring plan to inflict a crippling blow on his enemy. It involved first putting his men to work digging extensive earth fortifications around Richmond. This task was not popular with his troops, many of whom had expected to be made officers upon enlisting, not handed shovels.

"I fear," Lee sighed, "our soldiers have not realized the necessity for the labor they are called upon to undergo."

Lee needed the strong fortifications because he intended to risk leaving only 25,000 men behind them to defend the capital, while sending the bulk of his army against McClellan's in a surprise attack. It was a daring gamble. If McClellan realized Lee's plan, he could overwhelm the small body of defenders in the earthworks and seize Richmond.

Lee knew that he was risking the whole fate of the Confederacy on the gamble. If it failed, the war might possibly be lost by the end of the summer.

"The stake is too high," he wrote Jefferson Davis, "to permit the pulse to keep its even beat."

# 7

# "It Is Well This Is So Terrible"

On June 12, 1862, Lee sent a cavalry force under General Jeb Stuart on a dangerous raid around territory occupied by McClellan's army. He instructed Stuart to destroy Union wagon trains, seize their provisions, and return with information about Federal positions.

"Don't take unnecessary risks," he told Stuart. "Save and cherish your men and horses."

When the daredevil Stuart returned, he brought with him 165 prisoners, 260 captured horses, and seized Union supplies. His success created great enthusiasm in Confederate ranks, making Stuart a popular Southern hero.

At this time Lee received a letter from Mary, worried because their youngest son Rob, just turned eighteen, was determined to leave college and join the army. The news troubled Lee. Another son, Rooney, was already in battle as a cavalry major. Like Mary, Lee wanted Rob to stay in college.

"I am unable to judge for him," he finally wrote his wife, "and he must decide for himself. . . . I pray God to bring him to a correct conclusion." Rob promptly enlisted.

Lee pressed ahead with his preparations for what became known as the Seven Days' Battle, which began in Mechanicsville, Virginia. Lee telegraphed his general in charge of the fortifications in front of Richmond, "Hold your trenches tonight at the point of the bayonet if necessary."

It didn't prove necessary because McClellan believed, as Lee hoped he would, that Richmond was too strongly defended to take by a frontal attack. Instead McClellan fought a defensive battle against Lee's armies, withdrawing to fortifications on Malvern Hill. Lee, believing the Union forces to be demoralized by the retreat, ordered an attack on the hill.

The savage fighting produced great slaughter on both sides. Lee had erred in sending infantry to attack artillery positions. "It was not war," declared Confederate General A.P. Hill. "It was murder."

After the mistaken battle of Malvern Hill, ending on July 1, the Seven Days' Battle had cost over 20,000 Confederate casualties, while Union casualties were almost 16,000.

One reason the Seven Days' Battle had not gone as Lee had planned was some confusion among his generals. Unlike Grant, Lee relied on giving verbal instead of written, carefully specific orders. Also, Lee tended to stand apart from the battle once it had begun. He did not want to interfere with his generals the way Davis constantly interfered with him.

Lee preferred to consider the Seven Days' Battle a victory for him. "Under ordinary circumstances the Federal Army should have been destroyed," he wrote in his report to Davis. But he wrote Mary, "Our success has not been as great or complete as I would have desired, but God knows what is best for us."

The battle underscored for a grim Grant that the war was going to be a long, painful affair.

On July 11, 1862, Halleck was ordered to Washington to assume command of all the Federal armies. He ordered Grant to Corinth without telling him why. Responsibility for the Department of the Mississippi now fell upon Grant, although it was not until October that he was recognized as its commander.

Halleck sought to make Grant's new command as difficult as possible. He ordered Grant to draw the supplies needed from the hostile citizens of Mississippi with whom he and his troops were quartered. Halleck commanded him to take prisoners any who objected or throw them out of their homes: "Handle that class without gloves, and take their property for public use."

Grant was too decent to inflict that kind of pain on civilians. He refused to arrest or jail a single civilian during the entire war. Even if some might have been spies, Grant declared, "I deemed it better that a few guilty men should escape than that a great many innocent men should suffer."

Lee was made aware of Halleck's harsh intentions to punish Southern civilians. "I cannot believe that the enemy will carry out their threat of burning and laying waste to the countryside," he declared. "It is intended to intimidate. The sentiment in America will not tolerate it."

But when such violations of the rules of war had occurred, Lee snapped, "Those people are barbarians!" He ignored the fact that Confederate troops also committed atrocities.

Halleck sent 50,000 troops under Major General John Pope to join McClellan's forces. His plan was to catch and crush Lee between two Union armies.

Lee's forces clashed with Pope's in the second Battle of Bull Run on August 29. When Federals began attacking Lee's position, he ordered a battery commander to fire on them. The officer, worried about Lee's safety, protested, "But, General, as soon as we fire we will draw the enemy's fire right here."

"Never mind me," Lee said. He sat calmly on his horse Traveller while enemy shells answered the Confederate barrage.

Two gunners near Lee were blown to bits.

The fighting raged for several days. Lee constantly galloped along his lines directing the battle. When he halted Traveller near a gun battery, he was approached by a powder-blackened, clay-stained gunner. Accustomed to privates speaking to him, Lee asked, "Well, my man, what can I do for you?"

"Why, General, don't you know me?"

Lee squinted to decipher the features behind the blackened face, then smiled. "Hello, Bob," he greeted his son casually. "I'm glad to see you safe and well."

"General, are you going to send us in again?"

"Yes, my son," Lee replied. "You all must do what you can to drive those people back."

Then Robert Lee, Jr., returned to his battery to clean his cannon, while his father rode back to the battlefield in a light-falling rain.

On August 31 Lee received a painful injury when Traveller shied during a Federal attack, and Lee fell violently. Small bones in one hand were broken and the other wrist was sprained. Despite Lee's protests, both his hands were put in splints.

However, he led an attack on Pope's army while Stonewall Jackson attacked from the other side. The result was a Confederate victory in the second Battle of Bull Run. After suffering 14,500 casualties to Lee's 9,000, Pope was forced to retreat.

This Union defeat sent shock waves through the North and raised the spirits of the South. Washington panicked, fearful that Lee and Jackson would next attack the capital. Many Northerners felt that the cost of the war was becoming unbearable, with defeats dimming any hopes of an early end to it.

Some advocated stopping attacks on the South, and restraining the abolitionists, feeling that the Confederacy would then gladly make peace. Lincoln was aware that he needed some dramatic new military success to silence Union doubters.

But despite his victory at Bull Run, Lee's forces were in bad shape. Food supplies were low, horses exhausted, and all his troops were ragged and gaunt. Up to 3,000 of his men were now barefoot. Nevertheless Lee determined to drive on to Maryland and carry the war into Pennsylvania. His strategy was to compel the Federal forces guarding Washington to fight a decisive battle which Lee hoped to win and force an end to the war.

Asked later why he had not driven straight on to Washington, Lee replied, "Because my men had nothing to eat . . . for three days. I went to Maryland to feed my army."

On September 4, 1862, Lee did lead his army across the Potomac near Leesburg, threatening Baltimore and Washington. Washingtonians reacted with fright, demanding that McClellan beat off the Confederate attack before Lee could launch it.

Lee wrote Davis confidently, "The present position of affairs, in my opinion, places it in the power of the Government of the Confederate States to propose with propriety to that of the United States the recognition of our independence."

This could not be thought of as begging for an armistice, Lee felt, since his army was now in the position of inflicting injury upon the North. Moreover, if the North refused, guilt for continuing the war would be put on Lincoln.

Slowly recovering from his accident, Lee wrote Mary, "My hands are improving slowly, and, with my left hand, I am able to dress and undress myself, which is a great comfort. . . . The bandages have been removed. I am now able to sign my name."

Overconfident that his daring new moves were on the brink of success, Lee made a disastrous mistake. He split his forces, already outnumbered two to one, and sent each half to encircle the Northern force of McClellan four times as strong.

Lee dared risk this strategy because he considered McClellan an able but too cautious commander. "His army is in a very demoralized and chaotic condition," he told one of his generals, "and will not be ready for offensive operations — or he will not think so — for three or four weeks." Before then, Lee added, he hoped to be in Pennsylvania.

He was once more risking everything to win everything in a reckless gamble. Unfortunately for Lee, a Confederate general had used his notes of Lee's plans to wrap several cigars that he placed in his breast pocket. The package had fallen out, and was found by Union soldiers delighted with the cigars. Happening to glance at the paper wrapper, they realized what it was and quickly sent it to McClellan.

Guided by this exposure of Lee's plans, Mc-Clellan at once rushed his army to Antietam Creek. On September 17, 1862, he attacked Lee's forces in the Battle of Antietam in Maryland, the bloodiest one-day battle of the war. The Confederates fought desperately against the superior manpower of McClellan's army.

The battle began at dawn with a gigantic artillery bombardment of Lee's positions, and raged back and forth all day. A cornfield was fought over so bitterly that it changed hands several times. Two Union generals were wounded, one fatally. One Confederate general was killed and two wounded.

Lee lost 10,000 men to McClellan's 13,000, but Lee's casualties represented a far greater percentage of his army.

When what was left of a Confederate division under General John Hood retreated past Lee, he exclaimed, "Good God, where is the splendid division you had this morning?"

"Lying on the battlefield," Hood replied grimly.

"Gentlemen," Lee told his staff sadly, "we will not cross the Potomac tonight." He was forced to retreat to Virginia. In the retreat some 5,000 men strayed from his army.

Straggling was common in the Confederate

army. Soldiers felt free to leave their units to stop at a house for a drink, chat, or to write a letter. Officers rarely disciplined them.

"The greatest difficulty I find," Lee wrote Davis, "is in causing orders and regulations to be obeyed." But he himself never sought to enforce discipline. He regarded each Confederate soldier as a hero for whose support he felt grateful.

Grant now found himself being sabotaged by his own division commander, Major General John McClernand, an influential Illinois Democrat. McClernand had secretly gone to Washington to promote himself to Lincoln. He told the president that he could recruit a whole new army in Illinois and Indiana. In return he wanted a separate command, with authority to take this army and capture Vicksburg, Mississippi. That, McClernand hoped, would make him a war hero and boost his political fortunes.

The campaign against Vicksburg had already been assigned to Grant. But Lincoln found McClernand's proposal attractive. So McClernand went off to raise his army in the Midwest, with Lincoln's promise that Vicksburg should be assigned to him.

Informed, Grant wrote Halleck to protest.

"Two commanders on the same field are always one too many," he said later, "and in this case I did not think the general selected had either the experience or the qualifications to fit him for so important a position. I feared for the safety of the troops intrusted to him."

Even though Halleck disliked Grant intensely, he despised McClernand even more as a boastful politician — and a Democrat at that! — without military skills. Halleck therefore informed Grant that he had sole command of the Army of the Tennessee, and could fight the enemy "wherever you please." In effect that restored Grant's right to attack Vicksburg.

Lee was irked when, on September 22, 1862, Lincoln issued the preliminary Emancipation Proclamation, threatening to free slaves in those sections of the South which did not lay down their arms by January 1, 1863. The proclamation had no effect on the border states, Kentucky, Missouri, and Maryland, which had remained within the Union. In Tennessee and Virginia it affected only those unconquered areas still in rebellion.

Ironically, Lincoln was freeing slaves in areas where he could not enforce the edict, while leaving slavery in areas where he could. Nevertheless Lee viewed Lincoln's move as a shrewd attempt to make the Confederate struggle for independence seem a fight instead to preserve slavery (which in effect it was), while claiming the high moral ground for the North.

Back in Virginia, Lee regrouped his army and gave his weary men a much-needed rest until the end of October.

One day a staff officer found the usually impassive Lee in his tent with tears rolling down his cheeks. In Lee's hands was a letter from home informing him that his twenty-three-year-old daughter Annie had died in North Carolina after a brief illness.

But there was no time for mourning because word came that a huge Union army under General Ambrose Burnside was now massing near Fredericksburg, Virginia, preparing to attack Lee's forces. Burnside was replacing McClellan, whom Lincoln had removed from the Army of the Potomac for being too slow to resume the offensive against Lee.

Preparing to meet this new threat, Lee wrote Mary, "I tremble for my country when I hear of confidence expressed in me. I know too well my weakness, and that our only hope is in God."

Lee put 73,000 men in defensive positions around Fredericksburg. On December 13 Burnside made a series of attacks upon them with 113,000 Union troops. Lee's army threw up such devastating artillery fire that the battleground was strewn with 13,000 Union casualties. Lee's losses were 5,300.

A shaken Burnside withdrew his army.

Reviewing the bloody battlefield, Lee told his staff soberly, "It is well this is so terrible. Otherwise we should grow too fond of it."

Ironically, when the soldiers in blue and gray were not actually in battle against each other, they sometimes fraternized. They did so shortly after the Battle of Fredericksburg. On one side of the Rappahannock River a Union band was giving a camp concert for Yankee troops, playing patriotic songs.

Confederates on the opposite river bank gathered to listen, then yelled across a request for Southern songs. The Union band obliged with "Dixie," "Yellow Rose of Texas," and other Confederate favorites. Both armies sang all the songs together. Then the band played "Home Sweet Home," and both sides returned to their camps, thinking about the strange harmony between them.

Several months later the same troops fought each other to the death in the bloody Battle of Chancellorsville.

On another occasion pickets on both sides were shouting insults at one another across a field. One angry Yankee yelled a challenge to a rebel for a fistfight. Pickets on both sides declared a truce while the two boxers met and went at each other. After the fight they washed the blood off their faces and shook hands. Then they returned to their own lines, picked up their weapons, and both sides resumed shooting at each other.

In December 1862 Grant learned that his rival McClernand was on his way with the new army he had raised. Grant quickly prepared his own campaign against Vicksburg. The city had been strongly fortified with guns facing the Mississippi River. Until Vicksburg fell, the Union could not control this vital waterway. Grant knew that if he failed in his attempt to take Vicksburg, Halleck would promptly move to dismiss him or relegate him to the sidelines.

He worked out his plan for the Vicksburg campaign on his headquarters ship, during a social occasion on board for his officers and their wives. General James B. McPherson offered him a glass of liquor.

"Mac," Grant smiled, "you know your whisky won't help me to think. Give me a dozen of the best cigars you can find. I think by the time I have finished them I shall have this job pretty nearly planned."

Grant received good news in January 1863. It had become apparent to Secretary of War Stanton that McClernand was unfit to lead an attack on Vicksburg. Grant was authorized to take over his command.

He managed to position his troops directly opposite the strongly fortified city. But drenching rains bogged down his advance. His first attempt to take Vicksburg failed.

When Grant stopped at a house for a drink of water, the woman owner asked him in a tone of mockery whether he really expected to take Vicksburg. "Certainly," Grant replied.

"But when?" she sneered.

"I cannot tell exactly when I shall take the town, madam, but I mean to stay here till I do — if it takes me thirty years!"

Northern reporters visiting Grant's river-flooded camps found his soldiers suffering from typhoid, malaria, pneumonia, dysentery, infections, measles, and smallpox. Northern families were not aware that over half their sons in uniform who died were not killed in action, but died of diseases brought about by deplorable field conditions. Army medical knowledge and care in Civil War days were extremely poor.

The reporters pressed Grant for his military plans, but he refused to divulge them. "They pronounced me idle, incompetent and unfit to command men in an emergency," Grant wrote, "and clamored for my removal."

But Grant's iron determination and persistence endeared him to Lincoln, who supported his campaign against Vicksburg.

When General Burnside failed to take Fredericksburg, Lincoln replaced him as head of the Army of the Potomac on January 25. The president's hopes now rested on Major General "Fighting Joe" Hooker to outwit and defeat Robert E. Lee, who had only half the number of troops at Hooker's disposal.

Hooker divided his army into two encircling wings. By surrounding Lee's positions, he hoped to panic Lee into retreating from Fredericksburg. Then both halves of Hooker's forces would unite and pursue Lee to Richmond.

On April 29 Hooker launched his campaign with what he called "the finest army on the planet."

Lee meanwhile had fallen ill with a throat infection and heart pains. He wrote his daughter Agnes, who had hoped to visit him, "The only place I am to be found is in camp, and I am so cross now that I am not worth seeing anywhere. . . . Old age and sorrow is wearing me away, and constant anxiety and labor, day and night, leaves me but little repose. . . . The doctors have been tapping me all over like an old steam boiler before condemning it."

He nevertheless remained optimistic about the war, writing his wife, "I do not think our enemies are so confident of success as they used to be. If we can baffle them in their various designs this year . . . I think our success will be certain."

Shaking off his illness, Lee rode to a hill to watch Hooker's two Federal armies mass near the Rappahannock River. When they crossed, Lee seemed faced with two difficult choices. He could either fight two separate battles with fewer than 50,000 men, or save his army by retreating between the two Union forces.

But the wily Lee refused to behave as Hooker had expected. Leaving a force of only 10,000 troops to defend his lines, Lee led the main body of his army to attack one of Hooker's approaching columns. Hooker was confused by this unexpected bold strike at half his army. Fearful of Lee's reputation as a master strategist, he ordered a withdrawal to Chancellorsville.

Lee's risky gamble had saved the Confederate army.

Lee took another gamble. Leaving himself with only 14,000 men, he sent the rest with Stonewall Jackson to circle behind Hooker's position and fall upon it from the rear. Lee banked on Hooker's being too uninformed or too timid to risk a new attack on Lee's own weakened position.

Jackson made a night attack against Hooker on May 2. He was badly wounded in the left hand and arm, which a Confederate army doctor told him would have to be amputated. Jackson was asked whether he wanted it done on the battlefield.

"Yes, certainly, Dr. McGuire," Jackson replied calmly. "Do for me whatever you think best." His arm was amputated.

Informed, a grieved Lee wrote Jackson, "Could I have directed events, I would have chosen for the good of the country to be disabled in your stead."

Replacing Jackson with Cavalry General Jeb Stuart, Lee sent his forces to resume the attack on Hooker, and joined it with his last reserves. Colonel Charles Marshall described the Confederate troops as they fought: "The fierce soldiers, with their faces blackened with the smoke of battle, the wounded, crawling with feeble limbs from . . . the devouring flames, all seemed possessed with a common impulse."

On May 5 Lee threw all his forces into a final push to drive Hooker into the Rappahannock River. "Fighting Joe" did not wait for this final blow, but led his army back across the river in a driving rainstorm. By morning there were no Union forces left on Lee's side. In the Battle of Chancellorsville Hooker had lost over 16,000 men, Lee something over 12,000.

Once again a major Union campaign to take Richmond had come to nothing. Lincoln was devastated by Hooker's defeat.

"My God! My God!" he muttered, pacing his office in despair. "What will the country say?" He knew that many Northerners were growing weary of the war and would welcome peace overtures from the Confederacy to end it with a compromise.

A lull followed the bloody confrontation at Chancellorsville. Federal and Confederate troops began exchanging Northern coffee for Confederate tobacco in little toy boats made of planks they sailed across the Rappahannock. One evening rebel pickets even invited half a dozen Union pickets to attend a dance they were holding.

The dance was interrupted by a furious Confederate officer who ordered the Federals taken prisoner and jailed. The rebel pickets begged him not to do this since they had given a pledge of safety to the Yankees. The officer settled for reprimanding both rebels and Yankees, who were allowed to return to camp.

Not surprisingly, the impulse to fraternize was much stronger among ordinary Americans than any urge to kill each other.

# 8

# "Too Bad! *Too Bad!* TOO BAD!"

Although Grant's first attempt to take Vicksburg had been thwarted, largely because of stormy weather, his troops on the opposite side of the Mississippi continued to pose a dangerous threat to the city.

Lee decided that his best course of action was to mount a swift offensive in Pennsylvania, even with his reduced forces. He led an attack to the north. Lincoln replaced Hooker with General George M. Meade and sent him to stop Lee. Lee's hope that Lincoln would drain off part of Grant's army to join the Army of the Potomac was not realized. Lincoln's plans centered now on Grant's deep penetration into Mississippi.

"Whether General Grant shall or shall not consummate the capture of Vicksburg," Lincoln wrote an Illinois friend, "his campaign . . . is one of the most brilliant in the world."

But the South was jubilant because the Confederate army, despite inferiority in numbers and equipment, had proved more than equal to the Federal challenge. Jefferson Davis was irked, however, because Lee's victories had failed to compel Lincoln to sue for peace.

Lee now invaded Pennsylvania and replenished his army with civilian livestock and supplies which the Confederates badly needed.

Lee marched his army toward Gettysburg, Pennsylvania, after dark. His forces and Meade's suddenly encountered each other unexpectedly. The fighting began on July 2. The battles were bloody and fearful. Three times Lee's troops almost destroyed the Union forces before Meade was able to drive them off.

Lee brought up his only reserves to continue the battle. Next day he opened a furious artillery bombardment of the Union line on Cemetery Ridge, where Meade had assembled his entire army. Meade's cannon roared a deafening reply.

"The very earth shook beneath our feet," one Southern general wrote. ". . . For one hour and a half this most terrific fire was continued, during which the shrieking of shell, the crash of falling timber, the fragments of rocks flying through the air, shattered the cliffs by solid shot. . . . The splash of bursting shrapnel, and the fierce neighing of wounded artillery horses, made a picture grand and sublime."

When Lee rode past a wounded Union soldier, the Yankee pulled himself upright and shouted defiantly, "Hurrah for the Union!"

Lee sent Major General George Pickett to lead his division on one of the most famous charges of the Civil War. Pickett's men emerged from woods on a broad front, and raced over open ground toward the heavily fortified Union positions on Cemetery Ridge. In hand-to-hand fighting they almost succeeded in winning the ridge, but then were driven back with terrible losses. Over half failed to return to the Confederate lines.

Lee galloped out to rally the beaten troops into an orderly retreat to places of safety. He told one of his staff, "This has been a sad day for us, General — a sad day. But we can't expect always to gain victories."

He told the downcast Pickett, "Come, General Pickett, this has been my fight and upon my shoulders rests the blame. . . . If you had been supported properly by artillery, as you were supposed to be, you would have won the day." Shaking his head, Lee lamented, "Too bad! *Too bad!* OH, TOO BAD!"

In three days of fighting at the Battle of Gettysburg, over 22,000 of Lee's men were killed, wounded, or taken prisoner, compared to Meade's losses of over 17,000. Lee was forced to retreat back across the Potomac, fighting off Meade's army in pursuit. Pickett said years later, "That old man [Lee] had my division slaughtered at Gettysburg." For this Pickett never forgave Lee.

Gettysburg was considered the worst battle Lee had fought. Jefferson Davis was bitterly disappointed. He had ordered his vice president to contact Lincoln in the expectation that a great victory by Lee would force the Union to accept a truce.

But with Lee's army shattered at Gettysburg, on the same day Grant took Vicksburg, Lincoln refused to discuss any negotiations.

"It's all my fault," Lee wrote Davis remorsefully. "I thought my men were invincible." He offered to resign to make way for "a younger and abler man." Davis, however, had no intention of replacing his best and most popular general, who had come to symbolize the whole Southern cause.

If Jefferson Davis was disappointed at Lee's failure to defeat Meade, Lincoln was disappointed at Meade's failure to capture Lee and his army before they escaped back to Virginia.

"We had them within our grasp," Lincoln exclaimed. "We had only to stretch forth our hands and they were ours."

Lincoln fretted because his orders to Meade and other generals to attack and vigorously pursue Lee's forces were constantly met with excuses and delays. His generals, except for Grant, preferred to wage a defensive war from fortified positions as safer, risking fewer battle losses and casualties. Lincoln feared now that the war would go on indefinitely.

His worry was intensified by serious draft riots breaking out that month in New York City. Workers were infuriated by an act that allowed men to avoid being drafted by paying three hundred dollars, or sending a substitute to enlist for three years.

Over a thousand people were killed or injured in the workers' violent protest against "a rich man's war and poor man's fight."

They demanded conscription of black troops. They said, "A black man can stop a bullet as well as a white man." Troops had to be sent from Gettysburg to quell the riots. Soon afterward the Union army did begin recruiting black troops.

Grant, meanwhile, spent four months coping with rain, flooded bayous, and muddy roads before he could cross his army over to the eastern bank of the Mississippi, the same side as the enemy forces defending heavily fortified Vicksburg.

"I felt a degree of relief scarcely ever equalled since," he sighed. Now he was in a position to drive on the city.

Instead of wearing a handsome general's uniform like Lee, Grant still wore the plain uniform of a private, distinguished only by three stars on his shoulders. His generals shrugged off his modesty as one of Grant's eccentricities. They were also amused at his breakfasts, consisting of a cup of coffee and a cucumber sliced in vinegar. And any time he ate meat, it had to be cooked to a crisp because he still detested the sight of the bloody juice that reminded him of the tannery.

Planning his attack on Vicksburg, Grant was not, like Lee, guided by military tactics derived from studying famous European battles. He adjusted his tactics to prevailing conditions.

His son Frederick, thirteen, was now permitted to join him, accompanying Grant and sharing the hardships of each campaign.

When his troops reached Grand Gulf, Mississippi, on May 3 after a week of campaigning, Grant wrote that he had had "no change of underclothing, no meal except such as I could pick up sometimes at other headquarters, and no tent to cover me."

He ordered his troops to build a thirty-mile military road through swamps, and two three-hundred-foot floating bridges. Using them to cross almost impassable country, Grant attacked and captured the city of Jackson, forty miles east of Vicksburg.

Traveling ahead with his staff, minus tents, he slept on the porch of a house that had been made into a rebel hospital. It was filled with wounded and dying troops.

"While a battle is raging one can see his enemy mowed down by the thousand, or the ten thousand, with great composure," Grant wrote, "but after the battle these scenes are distressing, and one is naturally disposed to do as much to alleviate the suffering of an enemy as a friend."

He was about to order an attack on enemy troops stationed along the Vicksburg Road when a Union officer arrived with a message from Halleck. Grant was ordered to return north with his army to join other Union forces. Exasperated, Grant refused, declaring that the order had come too late and conflicted with his present position. The officer nevertheless demanded that Grant obey Halleck's order.

Suddenly Grant heard a great cheer on the right of his line. He saw one of his brigade commanders leading a charge upon the enemy. Grant immediately leaped on his horse and galloped off to join in the attack. The enemy fled.

The road to Vicksburg was thrown open to the Union forces.

Grant galloped along it in advance of his army. "Bullets of the enemy whistled by thick and fast for a short time," he wrote. On May 19, as his troops caught up to him, Sherman's forces joined him near Vicksburg. Grant ordered an assault which won a forward position.

On May 22 he ordered an all-out attack on Vicksburg itself. Fierce fighting ensued. Grant soon realized that he had made a mistake in throwing his infantry against heavily fortified positions, resulting in severe losses. Calling off the attack, he decided instead to lay siege to the city, digging in around it to starve it into surrender.

Grant and Sherman were both outraged when General McClernand sent a report to the Northern press blaming them for preventing *him* from taking Vicksburg. This was the last straw for Grant. He relieved McClernand from command of his troops.

Under a blazing Mississippi sun Grant set his

soldiers to work, digging deep, long trenches. He planned to keep extending them almost up to the Confederate trenches. One Union picket captain shouted an offer to a Confederate picket captain. If the rebels abstained from shooting Union trench-diggers, the Yankees would pledge not to shoot Confederate trench-diggers.

"All right," the Confederate captain shrugged. "You Yanks will have the place soon anyway."

A Confederate army sent by General Richard Taylor suddenly appeared, attacking Union lines upstream from Vicksburg. The Union defenders were a few newly enlisted black regiments. Fighting valiantly, they repelled the assault. Grant reported to Lincoln that they had acquitted themselves extremely well, the first acknowledgment that blacks could make good fighting men, not just army labor gangs.

Grant was impatient to take Vicksburg, considering the big city worth "the capture of forty Richmonds." Having to wait out a long siege, he eased his disappointment and boredom by beginning to drink heavily in early June. His friend and aide, Rawlins, urged him to let the bottle alone in order to keep a clear head for the coming campaign. But Grant had a number of lapses, and was seen drunk by his generals and reporters.

All protected him, fearful that if a news story about it got out, Grant might be relieved of his command.

Both sides sought to dig under the other side's trenches in order to blow them up. Close enough to talk, rebels and Federals often chatted casually with each other. Union soldiers would offer their hardtack or coffee for Confederate tobacco. Sometimes instead of exchanging these, one side would throw over hand grenades, and the other side would toss them back.

The siege was slowly starving civilians as well as soldiers in Vicksburg. One woman said, "I have never understood before the full force of these questions — what shall we eat? What shall we drink? And wherewithal shall we be clothed?"

Many civilians and soldiers survived on mule meat.

At last on July 3, after a siege of forty-seven days, Confederate General John Pemberton ran up a flag of truce to ask for terms. Grant had served in the same division with him in the Mexican War. At first Grant insisted upon unconditional surrender.

"I assure you, sir," Pemberton snapped, "you will bury many more of your men before you enter Vicksburg!"

Grant finally agreed to release Pemberton's 31,000 troops on parole without weapons, instead of shipping them up the river to Northern prison camps. Pemberton surrenderd the city.

On the Fourth of July Grant celebrated Independence Day by marching into Vicksburg with his troops.

"Our soldiers were no sooner inside the lines," Grant reported, "than the two armies began to fraternize. Our men had full rations from the time the siege commenced to the close. The enemy had been suffering particularly toward the last. I myself saw our men taking bread from their haversacks and giving it to the enemy they had so recently been . . . starving out."

The North was beside itself with excitement as the twin Fourth of July victories at Gettysburg and Vicksburg were announced. Although Gettysburg had been the greater battle, Grant's winning control of the Mississippi made him the hero of the day. Independence Day fireworks burst over every Northern town and city as Northerners screamed with delight. Enthusiastic chants were raised: "Grant for President!"

Lincoln expressed delight that at last he had found a general who "had the habit of victory," who had in fact twice captured a whole enemy army. Such elaborate praise was most welcome to the bearded general once despised as a civilian failure. Lincoln rewarded Grant by making him a major general in the regular army, the highest rank then available.

While Grant's star ascended, Lee's fell. Lee now told Davis, "The number of desertions is so great and still continues to such an extent that unless some cessation of them can be caused I fear success in the field will be seriously endangered."

To stem desertions, Lee offered amnesty to all Confederates absent without leave who returned within twenty days.

A month after the Vicksburg victory Grant, riding a spirited horse, reviewed one of his armies. Riding on to New Orleans, which had been captured in April, he was thrown suddenly when his horse reared at an approaching streetcar, then fell on Grant. In great pain from a badly swollen leg and side, he was carried back to Vicksburg in a litter.

He lay bedridden for almost two months as Julia rushed to his side. A flood of rumors suggested that alcohol had played a role in Grant's accident, especially since it was well-known that he was a superb rider.

Lee was also disabled, with rheumatism, the result of too many stormy days in the field. He now could not ride Traveller along with his regiments, but had to follow in a wagon. To add to his displeasure, a new mess steward butchered a pet hen to provide a fine meal for an important visitor, leaving Lee without his morning egg.

Far more worrisome was news that his son Rooney had been captured and was being threatened with hanging in retaliation for the Confederacy's threatened execution of two Federal soldiers as spies. To Lee's relief, neither side went through with the hangings. Lee fervently hoped that Rooney might soon be included in a prisoner exchange. His son's capture had seriously affected the health of both Mary Lee and Rooney's wife.

On September 19 a bloody battle at Chickamauga sent the Federal army reeling back to Chattanooga in defeat.

Fearful of losing Tennessee, Lincoln and Stanton decided that a drastic change in Union army leadership was needed to save the situation. Grant was given command of a newly created Military Division of the Mississippi.

For the first time he would not be under the thumb of Halleck, whose orders he was sometimes able to ignore. Now he was authorized to develop his own military strategy.

On October 23 Grant broke through to Chattanooga to hold off the attacking Confederate army. His arrival inspired the besieged Union troops. The atmosphere changed from one of expected defeat to enthusiastic optimism, especially after Grant distributed full rations to the hungry soldiers.

"We began to see things move," one officer reported. "We felt that everything came from a plan. Grant came into the army quietly, no splendor, no airs, no staff. He used to go about alone. He began the campaign the moment he reached the field. Everything was done like music, everything was in harmony."

Leading his troops against great odds, Grant won

the battle of Chattanooga, driving the Confederate forces back to Chickamauga.

On November 19, 1863, a national cemetery was dedicated at Gettysburg by Lincoln. Grant was deeply moved when he read the president's brief two-minute speech, humbly venerating the thousands of dead Federal soldiers who had given their lives at Gettysburg so that the Union might endure. The speech was only casually noted by the press, but was later to become famous as the Gettysburg Address.

Lincoln wrote Grant on December 8, "I wish to tender you, and all under your command, my more than thanks, my profoundest gratitude for the skill, courage, and perseverance with which you and they, over so great difficulties, have effected that important object [the Chattanooga victory]. God bless you all."

Grant's reputed alcoholism mattered not at all to the president, as long as Grant kept winning battles.

Congress also gave him a vote of thanks, and voted him a gold medal. Citizens of his home state presented him with a diamond-hilted sword in a gold scabbard engraved with the names of the battles in which Grant had fought. Rumors began to fly about nominating him in the 1864 presidential campaign.

"Nothing likely to happen would pain me so

much," Grant declared on December 17, "as to see my name used in connection with a political office. I am not a candidate for any office nor for favors from any party."

A Chicago businessman reported Grant's disclaimer to Lincoln. The president replied, "My son, you will never know how gratifying that is to me. No man knows, when that presidential grub gets to gnawing at him, just how deep it will get until he has tried it. And I didn't know but what there was one gnawing at Grant."

By this time Lee's army was literally in rags, half-starved, and badly lacking essential supplies and equipment. Southern civilians were faring little better, suffering from shortages of food, clothing, medicine, and in many cases houses, where these had been destroyed by Union artillery fire. Yet so fierce was the loyalty of most to the Confederacy that they continued to support the struggle, whatever the cost.

Added to Lee's anxiety over being able to keep his troops an effective fighting force was his worry over where Grant would strike next.

Knowing his reduced numbers made it more essential than ever to outthink Grant, Lee tried to read his enemy's mind and anticipate the next Union thrust. He guessed that Grant would try to move on Richmond through the forbidding country of the Wilderness. This was a dense forest a dozen miles wide and half a dozen miles deep, along the southern bank of the Rapidan River. Entangled vines, creepers, and heavy undergrowth made it impossible to see farther than twenty yards. The Confederate troops knew the area well, but it would be a blind maze for the Northerners. Lee's guess was an accurate one, and soon resulted in one of the most terrible battles of the Civil War.

Grant, traveling through Tennessee and Kentucky, found that his fame attracted Southerners curious to see him. They expected him to be the oldest member of his staff. Grant, who was only forty-one, would let his fifty-four-year-old, gray-haired medical director take the spotlight.

"The crowds would generally swarm around him," Grant smiled, "and thus give me the opportunity of quietly dismounting and getting into the house."

He was alarmed when word reached him from Vicksburg that his son Frederick, who had accompanied him on the campaign to take that city, had contracted a disease there and was dangerously ill in a St. Louis hospital. Grant received permission from Lincoln to leave the front to visit his son, on condition that he keep his headquarters with him, directing his generals from horseback or wherever his journey took him.

Lincoln did not want Grant's hand removed from

control of the war for a moment. If the war was not won before the fall elections of 1864, a stalemate might give the Democrats a good chance to win the White House with a peace program.

It was all up to Grant.

## 9

# The Noise of Battle

Lincoln asked Grant to come to Washington for a promotion that would put him in complete command of the entire land forces of the United States.

On March 8, 1864, Grant arrived at Willard's Hotel with his son Frederick, now fourteen and recovered. Grant came unattended by any staff, and carried his own suitcase. He signed the hotel register simply as "U.S. Grant and son, Galena, Illinois."

Because of his field-rumpled uniform without any general's insignia, the clerk took him for a lower-grade officer and showed him up to a dingy fifth-floor room. Grant considered this quite satisfactory, and chose to remain unidentified.

But journalist Richard Henry Dana spotted him and reported Grant's arrival, describing him as an "ordinary scrubby-looking man with a slightly seedy look." Grant's preference for anonymity was quickly swept aside as word spread that the great military hero of the Civil War was in town.

Crowds jammed Willard's Hotel to see and shake the hand of Lincoln's favorite general. Cheered and mobbed when he and his son entered the dining room, Grant endured shaking all the hands pressed on him until he was finally allowed to dine in peace.

He could not move anywhere in Washington without being applauded and cheered. Lincoln gave him a public reception at which Grant was promoted to second in command only to the commander-in-chief, Lincoln himself.

This was the first time Grant had met the president face-to-face. Lincoln was impressed with Grant's modest manner.

"General Grant," he declared, "because of the nation's appreciation of what you have done, and its reliance upon you for what remains to be done in the existing great struggle, you are now presented with this commission constituting you lieutenant-general of the Army of the United States."

"It will be my earnest endeavor," Grant replied, "not to disappoint your expectations. I feel the full weight of the responsibilities now devolving on me."

Grant told Julia that his only regret at accepting the promotion was that it bound him to Washington, instead of allowing him to continue serving in the field.

Almost immediately there was renewed speculation about Grant as a presidential candidate, possibly even replacing Lincoln. Grant was disturbed by this distraction from his military mission. He wrote an Illinois friend, "I am not a politician, never was and hope never to be. . . . My only desire is to serve the country in her present trials."

Congressmen had created the rank of lieutenant general for Grant at Lincoln's insistence. But many expressed concern about turning the country's armies over to a reputed alcoholic. Accordingly, Congress gave Grant a new chief of staff — his friend John Rawlins, known to be able to keep him sober.

In Lincoln's consultations with Grant, the president said he had no wish to dictate war plans as he was not a military man. However, he expected to offer suggestions that Grant would be free to follow or ignore. In other words, unlike Jefferson Davis's attempt to run the Army of Northern Virginia with Lee in a subordinate role, Lincoln was turning over total control of all the Union armies to Ulysses S. Grant.

Grant told the president that the cavalry had not been used to the best advantage so far in the war. He wanted the best man he knew in the army for that command — General William Tecumseh Sherman. Sherman was immediately sent for and put at the head of the Army of the Potomac's cavalry corps.

Bringing Julia and the children to Washington, Grant made his headquarters in a plain brick house. Tents were erected in the yard for his staff. Riding a big bay horse at a gallop, Grant visited troops in the field. Now he had over half a million soldiers under his command.

The soldiers he reviewed saw a slouchy, round-shouldered officer with a short, bristly red beard and flinty look. Riding past one celebrated brigade of Wisconsin troops, Grant slowed his horse to a walk. Then he took off his hat and bowed to the soldiers, in honor of their famed fighting ability.

When he reached Meade's headquarters, the unkempt commanding general in a private's blouse with only plain stars on his shoulders stared at Meade's personal banner, which bore a golden eagle and silver wreath.

"What's this?" Grant grunted to his staff. "Is Imperial Caesar anywhere about?"

Now, for the first time, General Ulysses S. Grant, commanding all the Union armies, would be pitted directly against General Robert E. Lee.

The brusque, sloppily dressed, tenacious Northern son of a tanner would have to match wits with the courteous, elusive Southern gentleman resplendent in his uniform. The whole country prepared to watch the classic duel between the two generals.

Lee was fully aware that he would have a tough time outfighting Grant. General James Longstreet warned him gloomily, "That man will fight us every day and every hour till the end of the war."

Lee was now more handicapped than Grant in their confrontation because Grant's now unlimited powers allowed him to shift around Union armies as he wished. Lee, on the other hand, had command only of the Army of Northern Virginia. Even these decisions were subject to Davis's approval, as were those of the other Confederate armies. In a real sense Grant's opponents were both Lee *and* Jefferson Davis.

Grant's problem was not only defeating Lee's forces and occupying the Confederate capital. He felt he would also have to occupy the whole South, subduing the will of hostile Southerners.

Grant planned to wage battles simultaneously in all theaters of the war, while keeping Northern losses as low as possible. But the advantage, he knew, would be with the Confederate commanders because attacking forces usually suffered three times as many casualties as a defending army.

Lee's strategy, meanwhile, was to keep threatening to attack Washington. This compelled Grant to keep much of the Army of the Potomac there instead of using these forces for a drive on Richmond. But he ordered Meade to take some of that army south.

"Lee's army will be your objective point," he told Meade. "Wherever Lee goes, there you will go also."

At the same time he ordered Sherman to march south from Chattanooga to capture Georgia.

Grant's plan was for Meade to keep Lee's army so busy it would not be possible for Lee to detach troops to help fight off Sherman's campaign in Georgia.

Grant knew that, despite the North's material advantages, time was of the essence because time was on Lee's side. The longer Lee could drag out the war, the more discouraged Northerners would get. They would listen to the peace forces demanding an end to the bloody war.

As a campaign issue in the fall, it could defeat Lincoln and the Republicans for a second term. A Democratic administration would agree to a peace that would leave the Confederacy — and slavery — intact.

Grant put a stop to prisoner exchanges with the South. Because there were many more Confederates captured than Federals, he decided that the South, hard-pressed for manpower, had more to gain by the exchanges. Both sides consequently needed to build larger prison camps.

The worst Southern camp was Andersonville Prison in Andersonville, Georgia, where 30,000 Union captives were herded together without shelter. Up to 15,000 died of neglect. In the North, Confederate captives were crowded together on swampland in Elmira Prison in Elmira, New York. They suffered from bad food and brutal guards. Prisoners on both sides got only whatever was left after the troops and civilians were fed, clothed, and given medical care.

Confederate troops outside the prison camps were not much better off. Lee felt despair that his men had to get along with inadequate food and clothing, worn-out shoes, and the lack of even tent shelter. It pained him to watch his men shivering in their threadbare uniforms, and see the bloody tracks their often bare feet left in the snow.

The Confederacy now did not have enough manpower to keep its army up to strength and run its war plants, so supplies for the rebel troops grew increasingly scarce. Consequently many hungry, ragged, exhausted rebels deserted, reducing Lee's troops to almost half their original number.

In contrast Grant received almost everything he asked Lincoln for. Preparing to open his major campaign against Lee, he expressed his appreciation to the president. "Should my success be less than I desire and expect," he wrote Lincoln, "the least I can say is, the fault is not with you."

Grant was aware that Lee's strategy was to move his troops around skillfully to avoid heavy casualties. To pin Lee's forces down, Grant decided on coordinated heavy attacks that would keep them on the defensive, while the Northern armies sought to inflict crippling losses.

To thwart Grant's drive to capture Richmond, Lee counted on the Wilderness the Union army would have to drive through to serve as a spider's web to entrap the Federals.

Lee planned to slash Grant's Army of the Potomac to pieces when it crossed the Rapidan and tried to advance through the Wilderness jungle. Preparing for his first direct battle against the new enemy leader, Lee wrote his father-in-law, "If victorious, we have everything to live for. . . . If defeated, there will be nothing left for us to live for."

To make Grant's task more difficult, his forces could not take sufficient food and supplies with them on the campaign, and would have to rely upon foraging off the hostile countryside. Lee's troops, operating in their own territory, were being supplied from Richmond.

In April Grant ordered Sherman to begin his attack upon Atlanta and Savannah, then advance on Lee's rear.

Alarmed by Grant's fierce campaigns, Confederate General James Longstreet suggested to Lee that he transfer his own troops in the West to join Lee in attacking Washington.

"I believe, however," Lee now decided, "that if Grant could be driven back and Mississippi and Tennessee recovered, it would do more to relieve the country and inspirit our people than the mere capture of Washington."

Lee narrowly missed having Grant in his hands as a prisoner in May 1864. When Grant returned to his field headquarters by special train after a visit with Lincoln, he observed a heavy cloud of dust obviously made by charging cavalry. After his one-car train stopped at a junction, he learned that only a few minutes earlier Confederate Colonel John S. Mosby had led his cavalry regiment in pursuit of Federal cavalry.

Had Mosby seen the special one-car train, he might have suspected that it carried an important Union leader. If he had let the Federal cavalry escape and attacked the train instead, the capture of Grant would have changed Civil War history.

As Grant prepared to launch his Wilderness campaign, he pitched his headquarters tent in a meadow with Meade's forces. He felt good being back in the field, joining the fighting, instead of remaining bottled up in Washington. Calmly whittling some branches and puffing at a cigar, he issued orders to his generals to deploy their troops.

Lee, who had observed Union army movements from a hill across the Rapidan, deliberately refrained from attacking Grant's 115,000-man force as it crossed the river on May 5. He waited until the Federals had entered the Wilderness, which Lee had chosen as his battlefield.

At Lee's signal, 65,000 Confederate troops attacked the Union army. The jungle made Grant's numerical superiority of little value. In the fierce battle the Northerners, fighting blindly, often shot each other instead of the enemy.

Soldiers on both sides became isolated from their units. They fired at any bush that moved as they sought to locate their own lines. Whole regiments disintegrated. Scores of Federals stumbled into Confederate lines and were captured, while Confederates blundering into Union lines were taken prisoner. Anywhere soldiers looked, they saw only trees, bushes, and blinding gunsmoke. The deafening noise of battle set up a frightening din.

In the two days of the Battle of the Wilderness, Grant lost over 17,000 men, Lee over 7,500. Lee's smaller losses were still severe because they represented a larger proportion of his forces than Grant's did. Under cover of night Lee withdrew his troops. Although Grant had achieved no victory, he had accomplished his objective of forcing Lee on the defensive.

Meanwhile Lee anticipated Grant's next move — an advance on Spotsylvania in the southeast. He raced his forces to Spotsylvania to get there first. Lee proved correct, and had his forces in position to attack when Grant showed up.

For six days Grant tried to break Lee's lines. Much of the fighting was fierce hand-to-hand combat in the forest, with bayonets, swords, and muskets used as clubs. Confederates and Federals engaged in deadly wrestles. Wounded soldiers refused to retreat, continuing to fight as they bled.

In effect, soldiers on both sides were fighting blindfolded. Troops charged without knowing where the enemy was until they ran into them in the dense forest. Heavy smoke from the cannonades made vision even more obscured. Men lost all sense of direction. Whole divisions went astray and ran into murderous fire. Flames broke out in the forest, trapping some troops, burning them alive, and leaving them dead and dying in heaps.

Dismayed at the terrible price his men were paying, Grant shook his head sadly. "Meade," he grieved, "is all this killing really necessary?"

"Well, General," Meade shrugged, "we can't do these little tricks without losses."

One of Grant's generals warned him, "Lee will throw his whole army between us and the Rapidan, and cut us off completely from our communications."

"Oh, I am heartily tired of hearing about what Lee is going to do!" Grant exploded. ". . . Go back to your command, and try to think what *we* are going to do ourselves, instead of what Lee is going to do!"

At Spotsylvania Lee had blocked Grant's path to Richmond with only 61,000 troops compared to Grant's 102,000. But Lee's cost had been heavy — up to 8,000 casualties and 4,000 men captured. Grant's losses had been even heavier — 14,300 men killed, wounded, or missing.

And neither side had won anything worth mentioning.

"The world has never seen so bloody and so

protracted a battle as the one being fought," Grant wrote home to Mary, "and I hope I never will again." He acknowledged that Lee's soldiers had fought gallantly, but insisted that Lee was now fighting out of desperation.

He admitted to Stanton that it had been "impossible to inflict the heavy blow on Lee's army I had hoped."

But he told the president, "I propose to fight it out on this line if it takes all summer!"

Lee wrote Davis that every Federal attack had been repelled, and that his own army was still on the front.

"With the blessing of God," he declared, "I trust we shall be able to prevent General Grant from reaching Richmond."

On May 11 he ordered another attack on Grant's forces. The Federals beat it off so fiercely that Lee was stunned to find himself surrounded by Confederates running to the rear.

Pale with chagrin, Lee wheeled Traveller, shouting, "Shame on you, men! Shame on you! Go back to your regiments!"

Failing to halt their flight, he rallied other troops and began to lead them in a counterattack himself. But he was not permitted to charge at the head of his troops.

Seizing Traveller's bridle, General Gordon pulled Lee up.

"General Lee, you shall not lead my men in a charge!" Gordon insisted. "You *must* go to the rear, General!"

Reluctantly, Lee stayed behind. Seated on Traveller he watched the battle, still exposed to heavy enemy fire. As shells crashed around him, he ordered his staff to take shelter behind an old brick kiln, but refused to do so himself.

In a two-week battle the Confederates managed to hold off Grant's forces. General Jeb Stuart was killed in the fighting. Hostilities were forced to cease for five days by a drenching downpour that turned the forest into a swamp.

Lee wrote Davis that Grant's army "has been very much shaken." He had foiled Grant's attempt to take Spotsylvania and insert Union forces between Lee's army and Richmond.

Nevertheless Grant wrote Halleck that Lee's army was now "really whipped." He asked Halleck to tell Lincoln that only the constant downpours had forced the Union army to cease attacks, not any weakness or exhaustion on their part.

Riding along his lines, Grant was stopped at a house occupied by an old lady who told him, "It's been so long since I'd seen a Union flag that it does my heart good to see one again."

She revealed proudly that both her husband and son were somewhere in the Union army, if still alive.

"She was without food or nearly so," Grant

wrote, "so I ordered rations issued to her, and promised to find out if I could where her husband and son were."

As his army progressed southward, fighting off Lee's assaults, Grant grew increasingly confident that the Confederates were being defeated and knew it.

But Lee was determined that Grant would never take his beloved capital. "I begrudge every step he takes toward Richmond," Lee wrote Mary on May 23.

Coming down with an intestinal ailment, he was ordered to bed by an army doctor who told him he was too sick to continue in command. Why not summon Beauregard to take over for him?

"Nonsense!" Lee snapped. "Given one more chance, I can whip Grant. We must never let them pass us again! We must strike them a blow!"

He continued giving orders from his sickbed. Yet as his illness grew worse, Lee worried that he was beginning to wear out. "I am not fit to command this army," he sighed to an aide.

On June 1 Grant's forces captured the crossroads of Cold Harbor. Jubilant, he prepared to drive on to Richmond.

But Lee was waiting and prepared, his men dug into trenches. On June 3 when Grant opened his attack on the Confederate lines, his troops met a storm of rebel rifle fire. The dug-in Confederates mowed down advancing Federals, killing and wounding almost 7,000 in less than an hour. The shocked Union troops stumbled back from Cold Harbor in defeat.

Lee taught Grant a painful lesson at the Battle of Cold Harbor. Grant now realized that it was suicidal to attempt to capture a position where the Confederates were dug securely into trenches with clear lines of rifle fire.

Anguished, Grant ordered the Union army to retreat to their previous lines. "I regret this assault more than any one I have ever ordered," he admitted to his staff unhappily. "I regarded it as a stern necessity. But, as it has proved, no advantages have been gained sufficiently to justify the heavy losses suffered."

Wounded troops lay on the battlefield for three days, groaning for water and medical aid. Lee and Grant bickered in an exchange of notes over arrangements for a truce to rescue the wounded and bury the dead. By the time an agreement was reached, hundreds of the wounded had perished.

Northern hopes for a speedy victory were dashed by the Union defeat at Cold Harbor. Lincoln was depressed, aware that Northerners were growing weary of the war.

The president's reelection in November was now in serious doubt. General McClellan threw his hat in the political ring, calling for "new leadership to end the war and cut the Confederacy from the

*Robert E. Lee as a cadet at West Point.*

*Mary Custis, who became Lee's wife.*

*Stratford, Lee's birthplace.*

*An ad for the Carolina Clothing Depot that also crusaded against Lincoln's election.*

*Lee, on his horse Traveller, with his troops.*

*Jefferson Davis, president of the Confederacy.*

*Lee at the Battle of Fredericksburg.*

*The Battle at Shiloh.*

*A photograph of Stonewall Jackson taken
two weeks before his death.*

*Confederate and Union soldiers trading with each other
between the lines.*

*General Robert E. Lee with two of his officers.*

# Robert E. Lee

Head Quarters Army of Northern Va.
10th Apl - 1865 -

General Order
No. 9

After four years of arduous service marked by unsurpassed courage and fortitude, the Army of Northern Virginia has been compelled to yield to overwhelming numbers and resources

I need not tell the brave survivors of so many hard fought battles, who have remained steadfast to the last, that I have consented to this result from no distrust of them.

But feeling that valor and devotion could accomplish nothing that would compensate for the loss that would have attended the continuance of this contest, I determined to avoid the useless sacrifice of those whose past services have endeared them to their countrymen

By the terms of the agreement officers and men can return to their homes and remain until exchanged. You will take with you the satisfaction that proceeds from the consciousness of duty faithfully performed, and I earnestly pray that a Merciful God will extend to you his blessing and protection.

With an unceasing admiration of your constancy and devotion to your Country and a grateful remembrance of your kind and generous consideration for myself, I bid you all an affectionate farewell -

R E Lee
Genl

*Lee's farewell address.*

Union." General Rutherford Hayes, later to succeed Grant as president, wrote scathingly of McClellan, "Any officer fit for duty who at this crisis would abandon his post to electioneer . . . ought to be scalped!"

Many in the North, sickened by the heavy losses at Cold Harbor, were now calling Grant a "butcher." But Lincoln continued to have faith in his tough commanding general, whom he still hoped could and would win a quick victory.

Grant believed that the time had come now in the Civil War when both armies were seriously exhausted, but that whichever one pressed the fighting would be victorious. Counting on the heroism and endurance of his own men, he failed to appreciate that Lee's men were equally brave, and would continue fighting just as hard as his own.

Giving up his direct assault on Lee's lines, Grant maneuvered his troops in a swing around them, driving on the city of Petersburg. This was the last major city in the path toward Richmond. But when Grant reached the outskirts of Petersburg, he found Lee's forces already dug in around the city.

Grant ordered his own troops to dig in around Lee's lines, pinning the Confederates down. The two sides settled in for a long siege warfare thirty miles from Richmond on the James River.

Lee found that he was now losing more men to exhaustion and lack of decent food than to enemy fire. Scurvy, a disease caused by lack of fresh vegetables, was widespread.

Lee wondered if Grant realized that the most powerful weapon in the Federal arsenal was now simply time. It would destroy far more of the Confederate army than Union artillery.

# 10

# "What Is This All About?"

Grant decided on a new strategy. If he could take Petersburg, the Army of Northern Virginia and the Confederate government would begin to starve. That would force Lee's troops out of the trenches to attack the Union army.

On June 21 when Lincoln visited Grant's headquarters, Grant told him, "I am as far off from Richmond now as I shall ever be. I shall take the place, but as the rebel papers say, it may require a long summer's day."

Lincoln supported the plan to capture Petersburg, but asked Grant to do it with as little loss of life as possible. Northerners wanted no more bloodbaths like Cold Harbor, a rebel victory loudly trumpeted in the Southern press.

Grant wheeled some of his forces south of Petersburg to strike Lee's troops from the rear, getting between them and their supplies. He ordered General Phil Sheridan's cavalry to destroy the railroad and canal.

Lee quickly mounted a counterattack to relieve some of Grant's pressure on Petersburg and Richmond. He sent several corps under Lieutenant General Jubal Early and General John Breckinridge up the Shenandoah Valley to threaten Washington once more.

When Early's forces advanced to just four miles from the capital, Federal troops fell back before them. Civilians panicked as rumors of rebel atrocities flew around the city.

Families living on the outskirts in Maryland fled with their household goods. Panic intensified when the mail, telegraph, railway travel, and New York papers were cut off by Early's forces. All able-bodied males were pressed into the Washington militia.

Early sought to liberate 17,000 Confederate prisoners at Point Lookout, and add them to his army. In the nick of time three divisions sent by Grant arrived in Washington by sea. Suddenly facing superior numbers, Early prudently called off his attack and retreated, setting fire to Chambersburg as he did. Lee's final threat to Washington vanished.

Under fire in the trenches of Petersburg, Lee received melancholy news from his wife. Mary wrote that their home, Arlington House, which had been occupied by the Union army, had now been seized by the Federal government for nonpayment of taxes. Some two hundred acres around the house were being prepared as a national cemetery for the Union dead.

On the thirty-third anniversary of their marriage, Lee wrote Mary, "Do you recollect what a happy day thirty-three years ago this was? How many hopes and pleasures it gave birth to!"

An officer rushed in to warn Lee, "General, unless reinforcements are sent before forty-eight hours, God Almighty alone can save Petersburg and Richmond!"

"I hope God Almighty will," Lee replied somberly.

Despite Grant's pressure on Petersburg, Lee sent skirmishes against the Union forces to keep Grant busy fending them off.

Lee manifested no great regard for Grant's generalship when he wrote his father-in-law Custis, "His talent and strategy consists in accumulating overwhelming numbers." But Lee had no illusion about winning the war in the face of those numbers. He hoped that before he ran out of troops, Northern frustration with the prolonged war would force a political settlement upon Lincoln.

Grant had a surprise for Lee. He ordered Union soldiers who were Pennsylvania coal miners to dig a deep tunnel from the North's trenches to beneath Confederate trenches. At the end of the trenches 8,000 pounds of explosives were placed. On July 30, 1864, a fuse was lighted and a tremendous explosion sent a mass of rebel dirt, guns, men, and timbers into the air in a cloud of dust.

The explosion, much bigger than the one Grant had used to undermine the Confederate trenches at Vicksburg, broke open Lee's lines with a crater twenty feet deep and one hundred and seventy feet long.

Union soldiers who charged into the crater included 4,300 black troops who had never been under fire. But Union General James Ledlie, who was supposed to lead the attack, was not with his troops. Instead he was found cowering in a shelter, drunk.

His leaderless troops milled around inside the crater in confusion as Lee's troops rushed to the lip of the pit. They poured a murderous fire down upon the Union soldiers.

Lee rode to the front to direct the counterattack that made the crater a death trap for the attackers. Union casualties at the Battle of the Crater were almost 4,000, a third of whom were blacks. Grant was forced to order the attack through the crater called off. He later called the fiasco "the saddest affair I have witnessed in this war," and frankly labeled it "a stupendous failure." General Ledlie was discharged in disgrace.

The Battle of the Crater marked the first time Lee's army had encountered Northern black soldiers. A rebel report admitted, "Our men, inflamed to relentless vengeance by their presence, disregarded the rules of warfare which restrained them in battle with their own race, and brained and butchered the blacks until the slaughter was sickening."

* * *

Grant was angered by Early's burning of Chambersburg, Pennsylvania, in the rebel retreat from Washington. He ordered Sheridan to retaliate by taking troops raging through the Shenandoah Valley and reducing it to a "barren waste." He told Sheridan, "Put yourself south of the enemy and follow him to the death!"

Similarly, he sent Sherman to Georgia to attack Atlanta and "push the enemy to the very death!"

When Grant spent four days in Washington conferring with Lincoln and Stanton, Stanton wanted him to cancel his orders to Sheridan and Sherman as much too bloodthirsty. But Lincoln intervened, saying that Grant's orders were exactly what he wanted done. He wanted the war over as quickly as possible.

Lee, learning that Sherman's troops were marching through Georgia, the heart of the Confederacy, was concerned about the potential loss of food supplies for his army. Asked whom he considered the Confederacy's best friend, Lee replied wryly, "The only unfailing friend the Confederacy ever had was cornfield peas!"

The siege of Petersburg went on endlessly. During the stalemate, insults hurled across the lines gave way to good-natured conversation out of boredom. Rebels and Yanks even washed clothes together in the streams, and organized footraces and wrestling matches. Bored officers did not interfere, feeling that the interplay was harmless and raised morale.

The men on both sides knew that in time they would receive orders to start killing each other again. But until then, well, they were all fellow Americans, weren't they?

Grant himself didn't mind. His main object for the time being was to keep all of Lee's forces pinned in place so that they couldn't go south to fight off Sherman in Atlanta. The capture of Petersburg, he was convinced, would come in due time.

A visitor from Washington told Grant that there was increasing talk of running him for president in place of Lincoln.

"They can't do it!" he growled, hitting the arms of his camp chair with clenched fists. "I consider it as important to the cause that he should be re-elected as that the army should be successful in the field!"

Grant carefully followed campaigns of his more than a million men operating on battlefields thousands of miles apart.

"The art of war is simple enough," Grant told one of his staff. "Find out where your enemy is. Get at him as soon as you can. Strike at him as hard as you can and as often as you can, and keep moving on."

On September 2 an advanced echelon of Sherman's army fought their way into northern Atlanta, while Sherman led his major forces in an attack south of the city. Confederate General John B. Hood realized resistance was futile, and evacuated his troops from the city, blowing up ammunition dumps behind them.

Sherman's troops marched into Atlanta triumphantly, bands playing, past buildings wrecked by heavy Union bombardment. The Federals lowered the Confederate flag over the city hall, and raised the Stars and Stripes. Sherman followed Hood's retreating forces for a few miles, then let them go, to give his own army time to rest and refit in Atlanta.

Jubilant at the news, Grant galloped to meet Sheridan in the Shenandoah Valley to spur on that campaign. On September 19 Sheridan led his troops against Early's army, winning a crushing victory. Following the fleeing rebels in hot pursuit, Sheridan stripped the valley of crops and cattle, destroying everything his troops could not carry away.

At this news Grant flung his hat up in the air. Congratulating Sheridan, he ordered a one-hundred-gun salute fired at Petersburg, with the guns aimed at the enemy. He ordered other commanders throughout the country to fire victory salutes also.

The Southern press began criticizing Lee for losing battles. He told Confederate Senator Benjamin Hill sarcastically, "We made a great mistake in the beginning of our struggle. . . . We appointed all our worst generals to command our armies, and all our best generals to edit the newspapers."

On October 1 Sherman asked Grant, "Why will it not do for me to destroy Atlanta and march across Georgia to Savannah or Charleston, breaking roads and doing irreparable damage? We cannot remain on the defensive. . . . I can make this march and make Georgia howl!"

Grant was hesitant, however, fearing an unfavorable reaction to Sherman's rampage could damage the Union cause. But he finally gave his consent, and Sherman started out on his famous march. Grant wrote him, "Great good fortune attend you!"

Cold weather made life in the Petersburg trenches miserable for both sides. Desertions increased. Confederate Lieutenant R. M. Collins wrote in his diary, "As we lay there watching the bright stars . . . many a soldier asked himself the question: What is this all about? Why is it that 200,000 men of one blood and one tongue, believing as one man in the . . . universal brotherhood of man, should in the 19th century of the Christian era be . . . seeking one another's lives? We could settle our differences by compromising and all be home in ten days."

In November Lincoln won reelection, helped by the popular victories of Grant, Sherman, and Sheridan. Grant asked Stanton to congratulate the president, writing, "The election having passed off quietly, no bloodshed or riot throughout the land, is a victory worth more to the country than a battle won."

On November 15 Sherman began his destructive march through Atlanta, his troops burning the city. Some believed that Sherman was motivated by a desire for revenge, after discovering how badly the Union prisoners at Andersonville had been treated.

Marching through smoke clouds, bands played as Federals sang "John Brown's Body." Sherman led his men down to the sea as the conflagration spread forty miles wide. At least 10,000 Atlanta slaves ran away to follow the Union army. Sherman estimated that he had inflicted one hundred million dollars worth of damage.

When the news flashed through Lee's army, thousands of anguished Confederate troops deserted to rush home to help their families, most of whom had been stripped of food and livestock. One family had pleaded with Union soldiers not to take their few chickens, the family's last source of food.

"The rebellion must be suppressed," a Federal replied, "if it takes the last chicken in the Confederacy!"

Sherman moved on to attack Savannah, Georgia. After a mine exploded under a Union officer's horse, Sherman ordered Confederate prisoners in front of his advance, either to dig up the mines or risk being killed by them. Lee's defending forces fled Savannah as Sherman stormed in, capturing the city on December 20.

Another bout of illness depressed Grant, but news of Sherman's victory in Savannah brightened him instantly.

"All well here now," he wrote Mary. "The good news of the capture of Savannah received from Sherman is worth a great deal. . . . The Confederates are very despondent and say, some of them, their cause is already lost."

Sherman telegraphed Lincoln, "I beg to present to you as a Christmas present the city of Savannah, with 150 heavy guns and plenty of ammunition, also about 25,000 bales of cotton."

Leaving a force to hold the city, he took his army north, as Grant had ordered, to attack the Carolinas at Lee's rear. As in Atlanta, he burned and looted plantations in his path.

Jefferson Davis was furious. He insisted that Lee take action to stop Sherman as quickly as possible. But Lee was still pinned down before Petersburg by Grant, and could not detach divisions to reinforce his generals south of him.

All through the cold winter he continued to live in a tent, explaining to Mary that he refused to disturb families in their homes simply to acquire more comfortable quarters. On Christmas Day Southerners provided a side of mutton for Lee and his staff. When it disappeared from the mess, Lee's upset steward told him he suspected the men of having taken it for themselves.

"If the soldiers get it, I shall be content," Lee

shrugged. "We can do very well without it. In fact, I should rather they should have it than I."

Jefferson Davis worried that with Tennesssee in enemy hands, the Confederacy could not get enough meat to feed both Southern civilians and the army. He wanted Lee to leave just enough force to protect Richmond, and strike out with enough divisions to recapture Tennessee.

Lee agreed that the situation was desperate, but pointed out that he had to defend Petersburg and Richmond at all costs, as the greatest immediate danger. Davis sent General Joe Johnston to do the job instead.

As the war dragged on, cautious negotiations were made at political levels for some kind of a restoration of peace.

"Let nothing which is transpiring," Lincoln wired Grant, "change, hinder, or delay your military movements or plans."

Grant assured the president there would be no armistice.

The war raged on.

Finding himself desperately short of men and supplies, Lee appealed to the Confederate Secretary of War, James A. Seddon.

"We have but two days' supplies," he wrote. "There is great suffering in the Army for want of soap." Noting an "alarming frequency of desertions," he asked that more reserves be added from boys fourteen to eighteen, and older men forty-five to sixty. He pointed out that he was being expected to hold more and more territory with fewer and fewer troops.

Meanwhile Jefferson Davis suddenly offered to send commissioners to a peace conference with Lincoln. Grant told Lincoln he believed the South was ready to stop fighting, and that a peace conference might now stop the war on the North's terms, ending further bloodshed. Lincoln agreed to receive the commissioners. Grant guaranteed them safe conduct, and sent them through his lines to meet Lincoln at Hampton Roads.

Soon afterward Lincoln visited Grant and reported that the conference had failed. The president had made it clear that the South first had to recognize that the Union had to be preserved in its entirety, and that slavery had to be abolished. The angry commissioners, who had expected to be received as representatives of an equal power, broke off the negotiations.

With hopes for a peaceful settlement gone, Lee's position grew increasingly hopeless. Many of his soldiers now had little food and no shoes. Confederate cities lay in ruins. Grant's forces had blown up Southern railroads and confiscated crops. There were few new troops to replace Confederate casualties, and desertions were now a serious problem.

"I do not know what can be done to put a stop to

it," Lee reported bleakly to the Confederate Congress. He appealed to that body to allow slaves to join the army, with the promise of immediate freedom to all who enlisted, and to their families at the end of the war. The Confederate Congress passed such a law, but it was too late to put it into effect.

Time, Lee realized grimly, was now clearly on Grant's side.

On February 17 Sherman took Columbia, the capital of South Carolina, and many of his troops set it on fire. Charleston was the next important Southern city to fall.

A discouraged Lee visited Richmond to see his family, who were now living in the Confederate capital. Lee's nephew George observed him pacing the floor, looking deeply troubled and thoughtful, obviously mulling over an important decision.

Lee's father-in-law, G.W. Parke Custis, asked him how the war was going. Lee replied that he had been compelled to ask the Confederate Congress urgently for provisions for his men.

"They don't seem to be able to do anything except eat peanuts and chew tobacco, while my army is starving!" he sighed.

He added, "Mr. Custis, when this war began I was opposed to it, bitterly opposed to it, and I told these people that unless every man should do his whole duty, they would repent it. And now . . . now they *will* repent!"

# 11

# Surrender at Appomattox

Jefferson Davis reluctantly gave Lee permission to write Grant asking for an interview to talk about an armistice. Returning to the field, Lee sent this request to Grant on March 2.

"Sincerely desiring to leave nothing untried which may put an end to the calamities of war," he wrote, "I propose to meet you . . . with the hope that an interchange of views may be found practicable to submit the subjects of controversy . . . to a convention for settlement."

He did not think Grant would agree. He wrote Davis, "My belief is that he will consent to no terms unless coupled with the condition of our return to the Union."

~ Grant replied to Lee briefly that he had no authority to meet "for a conference on the subject proposed. Such authority is vested in the president of the United States alone."

But since the line of communications had opened between them, Grant sent another, friendlier verbal message to Lee by an officer under a flag of truce. "Give General Lee my personal compliments," the officer was instructed, "and say to him that I keep in such close touch with him that I know what he eats for breakfast every morning."

That was also Grant's wry way of letting Lee know that Union intelligence was keeping tabs on all his moves. If Lee imagined he could slip away from Petersburg to reinforce Johnston, Grant wanted him to think twice.

Lee replied in the same wry tone through a Confederate emissary: "There must be some mistake . . . for unless you have fallen from grace since I last saw you [in Mexico], you would not permit me to eat such [miserable] breakfasts as mine without dividing yours with me." And to counter Grant's subtle warning, he told the Union officer receiving the message to present his compliments to Grant, and say that Lee knew perhaps as much about Grant's dinners as Grant knew about Lee's breakfasts.

Sensing the Union net closing in on them, Confederate General John B. Gordon asked Lee what they ought to do.

"There seems to be but one thing we can do," Lee replied quietly. "Fight. To stand still is death. It could only be death if we fight and fail."

On March 25, 1865, under cover of night, General Gordon led 10,000 troops in a fierce attack on the Union-held Fort Stedman, and captured it. But the victory was brief because an overwhelming counterattack by Grant forced Lee to order Gordon to withdraw with heavy losses. The last great offensive of the Army of Northern Virginia had failed.

"I fear now," Lee informed Davis, "it will be impossible to prevent a junction between Grant and Sherman."

He was right. Sherman joined Grant, and the two met with Lincoln at City Point for a conference. Although determined to fight the war to a bitter conclusion, all three agreed that once it was over, they would seek to overcome wartime hatreds, and try to "turn old enemies into friends."

Grant still had enough respect for Lee's shrewdness to worry that the Virginian might escape the Union cordon around him with his troops to continue the fighting.

"One of the most anxious periods of my experience during the rebellion," Grant wrote later, "was the last few weeks before Petersburg . . . I was afraid, every morning, that I would awake from my sleep to hear that Lee had gone . . . and the war [had been] prolonged another year."

With his staff assembled, Grant described his plan to place Sheridan's forces between the armies of Lee and Johnston. Sheridan expressed dismay at this suicidal mission. Taking him out of the headquarters tent, Grant told him in private to disregard those orders. They had only been intended for the ears of a Confederate spy known to be in the Union camp.

Grant's real order for Sheridan was to take part in an attack on the important road junction at Five

Forks, Virginia. Its capture would cut off Lee's army from Johnston's.

On March 31, in a drenching rain, Sheridan waged a powerful battle at Five Forks, decisively beating the Confederates.

On April 3 Petersburg was in Grant's hands.

Lee sent an urgent message to Davis: "I advise that all preparations be made for leaving Richmond tonight."

He retreated with his forces toward North Carolina, hoping to join Johnston's army opposing Sherman. Watching them flee, Grant did not order artillery brought up to bombard them.

"I had not the heart to turn the artillery upon such a mass of defeated and fleeing men," he explained later, "and I hoped to capture them soon."

On April 3 Lincoln joined Grant in Petersburg. The cigar-chewing Grant was handed a telegram that he read aloud to Lincoln. Richmond had been taken. The Confederate government had fled to Danville, Virginia.

To increase the bitter medicine for the Confederates, many of the first Union troops marching into Richmond were black. The newly freed blacks in Richmond greeted them with joy and pride.

But Lee's army still survived. Beaten and in flight, it was still dangerous. If it was to be destroyed, it first had to be caught. Grant joined the Union forces in pursuit.

Meanwhile Lee raced south to get the provisions

he needed at Appomattox, Virginia, and to join with Johnston's forces. Reaching Amelia Court House, he found ammunition and other supplies but, to his chagrin, no food. Halting his columns, he sent wagons into the countryside to find food. Lee appealed to farmers to feed "the brave soldiers who have battled for your liberty for four years."

Sheridan's cavalry, in vigorous pursuit of Lee's army, cut them off at Appomattox Court House. Meanwhile Grant was told that captured General R. S. Ewell had said he considered the war lost, and that the Confederate authorities ought to get the best terms they could in a surrender. Ewell felt that for every man killed now, someone was responsible for their "murders."

Ewell's statements made Grant thoughtful.

A message from Sheridan informed Grant that Lee was now well trapped between the Union armies. Sheridan urged Grant to join his cavalry and take charge of the capture.

On April 7 Lee received a Union courier under a flag of truce. In a letter to Lee, Grant wrote, "The results of the last week must convince you of the hopelessness of further resistance. . . . I feel that it is so, and regard it as my duty to shift from myself the responsibility of any further effusion of blood, by asking of you the surrender of that portion of the Confederate States army known as the Army of Northern Virginia."

Lee replied promptly, "Though not entertaining

the opinion you express on the hopelessness of further resistance . . . I reciprocate your desire to avoid useless effusion of blood, and . . . ask the terms you will offer on condition of surrender."

That night, lying down beneath some trees to sleep, Lee wondered what Grant's terms would be. Next day Grant wrote back that his one condition was that the men and officers surrendered must not take up arms any longer against the Union.

Lee mulled over Grant's reply for hours. Then he wrote back that he did not believe any emergency had arisen requiring the surrender of his army. But he was willing to meet Grant to discuss peace — in effect suggesting an armistice.

At this point his army was stationed a few miles east of Appomattox Court House. Conferring with his generals, Lee discussed the possibility of breaking through Grant's lines to escape. One attempt was made by some Confederate forces, but they were beaten back by Federals.

Facing a Union army under General George A. Custer, Confederate General John B. Gordon ordered Colonel Green Peyton to ride out with a white flag. Peyton protested that there was no truce flag. Exasperated, Gordon told him to wave a white handkerchief on a stick.

"I have no handkerchief, General."

"Then tear your shirt, sir!"

"General, I have only a flannel shirt. . . . I don't believe there's a white shirt in the army."

"Get *something* white, sir, and *go!*"

Peyton found a white rag and waved that.

Informed that his generals in the field were surrendering, Lee said sadly, "Then there is nothing left for me to do but to go and see General Grant, and I would rather die a thousand deaths."

On the morning of April 9 Grant, stationed in a farmhouse, fell sick with an agonizing headache. He rode off with some of his staff, hoping the ride might take his mind off the pain.

Before setting out, he ordered another attack on Lee's army, which had now diminished to only 8,000 men.

Lee, meanwhile, wrote to Grant again, saying, "I now request an interview in accordance with the offer contained in your letter of yesterday for that purpose." It was, finally, Lee's offer to surrender without specifically saying so.

Lee's aide Charles Marshall rushed the note to Grant's headquarters, only to find Grant absent. Learning that another Union attack on Lee had been ordered, Marshall urged that it be stopped. General Meade agreed to hold up the attack for an hour and a half to give Lee's letter time to reach Grant.

When it did, Grant jubilantly called off the attack.

"The pain in my head seemed to leave me the

moment I got Lee's letter," he wrote later. He immediately answered Lee, asking where the Virginian would like the meeting to take place.

A Southerner named Wilmer McLean offered his two-story brick farmhouse at Appomattox for the historic encounter.

As Lee prepared to ride there, a staff officer made a last-minute appeal to him not to surrender, but simply to disperse the army to fight guerrilla warfare in the hills.

Lee shook his head. "It would take years for the South to recover from the chaos," he said. "Federal cavalry would seep all over the South. And I myself am too old to go bushwhacking. No, our only course is surrender."

At 3:00 A.M. Lee dressed in a new, immaculate gray uniform, a red silk sash, and ornamented boots. He buckled on a dress sword with a carved hilt in a gold-embroidered scabbard. Mounting Traveller, he left for the McLean farmhouse accompanied by two generals. There they entered the parlor and conversed quietly while waiting for Grant to arrive.

Grant had left his camp that morning in "rough garb." He wore a dusty, unbuttoned, army-blue ordinary soldier's blouse for a coat, with only shoulder straps to indicate his rank. His pants and boots were mud-spattered. And, as usual, he wore no sword when on horseback.

"I must have contrasted very strangely," Grant admitted later, "with a man so handsomely dressed, six feet high, and of faultless form."

Accompanied by Sheridan and his staff, Grant made his way to the McLean house in the village of Appomattox Court House. He entered the parlor smoking one of his cigars.

When the two enemies at last came face-to-face, neither showed any expression as they shook hands. Observing the defeated Lee, Grant could feel only compassion for him. Lee's manner was quiet and reserved.

"What General Lee's feelings were I do not know," Grant wrote later. "As he was a man of much dignity, with an impassable face, it was impossible to say whether he felt inwardly glad that the end had finally come, or felt sad over the result, and was too manly to show it. . . . I felt like anything rather than rejoicing at the downfall of a foe who had fought so long and valiantly, and had suffered so much for a cause, though . . . one of the worst for which a people ever fought."

Grant considered it an unnecessary humiliation to demand of Lee and his officers the surrender of their swords, a symbolic gesture usual in such cases.

"I met you once before, General Lee," Grant said, "while we were serving in Mexico. . . . I have always remembered your appearance, and I think I should have recognized you anywhere."

"Yes," Lee replied, "I know I met you on that occasion and I have . . . tried to recollect how you looked, but I have never been able to recall a single feature."

After they talked about the Mexican War for a while, Lee said, "General Grant, I asked to see you to ascertain upon what terms you would receive the surrender of my army."

Grant replied that they were the same as in his letter — officers and men to be disarmed totally, placed on parole, and forbidden to take up arms again, with all armaments given up.

Lee nodded. "Those are about the conditions which I expected would be proposed."

"I hope it may lead to a general suspension of hostilities," Grant added, "and be the means of preventing any further loss of life."

Lee suggested that Grant put the terms in writing. Grant did so and handed them to Lee. The Virginian put on steel-rimmed spectacles and read the text. He was gratified that Grant had added a proviso that surrendering officers need not give up their side-arms, horses, or baggage.

"This will have a very happy effect upon my army," Lee responded, nodding. However, he asked that his cavalrymen and artillerymen, most of whom owned their own horses, also be allowed to keep them.

Grant agreed, knowing that most of Lee's troops

were small farmers who needed horses to put in new crops.

Lee signed the terms of surrender, and also offered to turn over a thousand or more Union prisoners held by the Confederates. He told Grant that they, and his own men, "have been living for the last few days principally upon parched corn, and we are badly in need of rations."

"I will take steps at once to have your army supplied with rations," Grant said promptly. He asked how many of Lee's men would need to be fed.

"Indeed, I am not able to say," Lee sighed. "My losses in killed and wounded have been exceedingly heavy, and besides, there have been many stragglers and some deserters . . . so I have taken no means of ascertaining our present strength."

"Suppose I send over 25,000 rations. Do you think that will be a sufficient supply?"

"I think that will be ample, and it will be a great relief, I assure you."

Just before 4:00 P.M. Lee shook hands with Grant, bowed slightly to the other officers, and left quietly.

On the porch he put on his hat and gloves, returned a salute from Federal officers, and called for Traveller. He mounted as Grant came out. The generals exchanged salutes and raised their hats. As Lee rode off, Grant said something to General Rufus Ingalls on the porch. His staff craned eagerly forward to hear his momentous words.

"Ingalls," Grant said, "do you remember that old white mule that Potter used to ride when we were in the city of Mexico?"

For Grant the Civil War was over, so why not talk of something else? The South had surrendered, and that was that.

But one of Grant's staff said to him in awed tones, "General, this day will live in history!"

At news of the surrender, Federal troops were delirious with joy. They yelled triumphantly and threw caps in the air. A hundred-gun victory salute began firing. But Grant quickly ordered a stop to the celebration.

"The Confederates were now our prisoners," he wrote later, "and we did not want to exult over their downfall." Saddened now by the tragedy of the long war, and pitying the defeated, Grant "felt like anything rather than rejoicing."

As Lee rode slowly through the ranks of his army, tears filled his eyes and trickled down his cheeks. His ragged troops at first cheered him, then sobbed as they waved their hats affectionately. Some threw themselves on the ground and wept.

"We love you just as well as ever, General Lee!" one rebel cried out. Another shouted hoarsely, "Let's go back to fighting and lick the Yankees!"

As Lee passed through his men, hands reached out to touch his boots and Traveller. Dismounting near a large oak tree, he told those who gathered around him, "Men, I have done the best I could for you. Go home now, and if you make as good citizens as you have soldiers . . . I shall always be proud of you. Goodbye, and God bless you all."

At 4:30 P.M. Grant wired Stanton, "General Lee surrendered the Army of Northern Virginia this afternoon on terms proposed by myself." The news touched off tremendous celebrations in Washington. Crowds rushed to the White House to cheer Lincoln.

An uproarious victory parade marched down Pennsylvania Avenue. After the parade Grant rode his horse down to the avenue to observe the thousands of excited people who still filled the sidewalks even though the parade was over. Recognizing him, the crowds cheered him enthusiastically. Grant simply smiled, nodded, and rode on.

Although Lee had surrendered only the Army of Northern Virginia, it was the main Confederate force, and without it further Southern resistance was doomed. The other scattered Confederate forces surrendered within six weeks. Only two commanders led their slender units into Mexico, rather than surrender, and offered their services to Emperor Maximilian against the French.

Thus ended the four-year Civil War in which some 600,000 young Americans, Northerners and

Southerners, lost their lives. As a percentage of the population of 1865, that was like losing four and a half million American soldiers today.

The defeat of the South marked the end of slavery in the United States. It also established the supremacy of Federal over state rights, and kept Americans one nation between the borders of Canada and Mexico.

# 12

# Lee After the War

$A$t age fifty-eight the future looked bleak for Lee. Over 360,000 Union soldiers had been killed, and their parents, widows, and children regarded Lee as responsible. They wanted him tried for treason and hanged or sentenced to a long prison term.

He was now in poor health. A doctor found that the illness he had suffered from during the war had not been rheumatism but angina, making him vulnerable to a heart attack or stroke.

His military career was finished, he had no job, and his home in Arlington was now Federal property. He could only go back to his family's rented house in Richmond. His wife Mary was now an invalid, living with their three unmarried daughters. Sons Curtis, Rooney, and Robert had emerged safely from the war, but with prospects as bleak as his own. Lee had only a few small investments on which to support his family.

He felt stunned and dazed. His whole world had been turned upside down. The Confederacy had vanished. His leader, Jefferson Davis, had abdicated. Lee's beloved Virginia and ten other Southern states were now out of the Union, at the mercy of what many Southerners feared would be a hostile Federal Congress bent on punishing the South.

Lee needed to get his invalid wife out of Richmond to a place where privacy would let him devote himself to caring for her. He wrote a friend, "I'm looking for some quiet little home in the woods." He searched for a small farm he could afford, hoping to compensate for the hungry Civil War years by enjoying "no end of cream, fresh butter, and fried chicken — not one fried chicken, or two, but unlimited fried chicken!"

Here he hoped to farm and write his war memoirs.

While visiting a cousin, Lee read the new President Andrew Johnson's proclamation of amnesty and pardon for Confederates who took an oath of loyalty to the Union. After much hesitation, Lee decided to do so, in order to regain his citizenship and remove any legal cloud over any farm he bought.

Returning to Richmond, he found that a Federal grand jury in Norfolk had just indicted him for treason, which was punishable by hanging. The South was shocked. Both Northern and Southern lawyers rushed to Lee's aid, offering to defend him.

"Well," he told friends, "it matters little what they do to me. I'm old and have but a short time to live anyhow."

But Lee sent word to Grant to remind him of the surrender terms agreed upon, under which

Grant had guaranteed that no further action would be taken against Lee and the Confederate troops. He asked Grant to obtain a presidential pardon for them.

Grant, indignant at Lee's indictment, warned President Johnson that he would resign from the army if Lee were arrested. He asked Johnson to issue pardons to Lee and all Confederates.

Johnson ignored the request. But word was passed to Federal prosecutors, who halted all treason proceedings.

News that Lee had applied for a pardon outraged some hard-line Southerners. They saw it as an admission by Lee that the Confederates had been wrong in fighting for independence. But Lee advocated seeking pardons as the quickest and most realistic way for Confederates to regain citizenship rights, and begin to elect their own officials. Millions of Confederates followed the example of the general they revered and trusted.

Many Northerners were furious that Lee and the Confederates could be forgiven so easily for their rebellion.

During the summer of 1865 Lee's daughter Mary told an influential Richmond woman bitterly, "The Southern people are willing to give Father everything he needs — except the chance of earning a living for himself and his family."

This remark was passed on to a colonel who reported it to trustees of a little, obscure Washington College in Lexington, Virginia. Nearly destroyed by war damage and almost bankrupt, it had only four professors and forty students. When the trustees met in August to nominate a new college president, Lee's name was proposed. He was unanimously elected to the post. The trustees were delighted when Lee accepted on August 24.

One reason for his acceptance was Lee's conviction that the only hope for the South now lay in Southern youth. They would need a superior education to lead the devastated states to a brighter future.

The college offered him a house and garden in which to grow vegetables, a percentage of tuition fees, and a salary of 1,500 dollars a year — if the trustees could raise it. For his inauguration on October 2, Lee rode the 108 miles to the college on Traveller, who had accompanied him out of the Confederate army. The trustees wanted to make a grand occasion of the inauguration. Lee insisted upon a simple ceremony.

Accommodations were readied for his family, who joined him at the college on December 2. Students flocked into Lexington to matriculate in a college headed by General Robert E. Lee.

When one student asked him for a copy of the rules of the college, Lee replied, ''We have only one rule here — to act like a gentleman at all times.''

On February 17, 1866, Lee was summoned to

Washington to testify before a Joint Committee on Reconstruction. The committee wanted to know what secessionists thought now about the Federal government. Lee said, "I have been living very retired, and have had but little communication with politicians."

Asked about the Radical Republicans' plans to amend the Constitution to give Southern blacks the vote, Lee said the South would object: "I think it would excite unfriendly relations between the two races." At the same time he said that many Virginians now believed in educating blacks.

His testimony angered many Northerners and Southerners alike.

"I am now considered such a monster," he wrote home, "that I hesitate to darken with my shadow the doors of those I love best, lest I should bring them misfortune."

As president of Washington College, Lee was able to attract large donations. These allowed him to add a chapel and ten new departments; expand graduate studies; and even offer an innovative new course for 1865 — photography. His accomplishments were so valued by the trustees that after his death the college was renamed Washington and Lee University.

A fair but strict administrator, Lee did not permit any of his decrees to be questioned. Once he decided to follow the example of the University of

Virginia and cut down the usual one-week Christmas holiday to Christmas Day alone. Angered, the whole student body threatened to boycott classes. Lee calmly announced that if they did, he would simply close the college.

There was no boycott.

By the second year of his college presidency, the enrollment had grown to three hundred students, many attracted by his fame. Lee found himself so impressed by the college's liberal education that he amazed an assistant professor by admitting, "The greatest mistake of my life was taking a military education."

There was speculation as to why none of Lee's daughters ever married. The explanation might have been his instruction to them: "Never marry unless you can do so into a family which will enable your children to feel proud of both sides of the house."

Some suspected that he was not eager to part with any of the daughters who worshipped him. His youngest, Mildred, said, "To me he seems a hero — and all other men small in comparison."

In 1868 President Johnson finally issued an amnesty for Lee and all Confederates. Hearing this while on vacation with Mary at White Sulphur Springs for their health, Lee simply shrugged.

A momentous event occurred on May 1, 1869. Grant, now president, extended an invitation to his former foe to visit him in the White House. It was a symbolic act by which Grant, through Lee, was extending a hand of friendship to Southerners to reunite the North and South. Lee accepted. When he and Grant sat down for a private conversation, it went largely unrecorded.

When Lee took his leave, the two former enemies shook hands and never saw each other again. Lee had not much longer to live. Suffering a stroke after a walk back from chapel in the rain, he lay in bed for days. Sometimes he grew delirious, imagining he was back in the war.

On October 12, 1870, only five and a half years after Appomattox, Lee gave his last order at age sixty-three.

"Strike the tent," he whispered. The tent of his life was to be taken down in preparation for moving on to his next destination. Then he closed his eyes and died.

All of the South was plunged into mourning. Most Southern states declared January 19, Lee's birthday, a legal holiday.

He was buried beneath the campus chapel. Each year thousands came, and continue to come, to pay their respects at the grave of the most famous Southern war hero since Lee's own lifelong idol, fellow Virginian George Washington.

# 13

# Mr. President

At forty-three, Grant, the younger general, still had twenty years and a tumultuous life ahead of him after Appomattox.

When he arrived in the capital on April 14, 1865, Lincoln received him with deep emotion. He invited the Grants to attend the theater that evening with the Lincolns.

Grant, knowing that Julia could not stand the imperious Mary Todd Lincoln, whom she had met at City Point during the war, thanked the president but pleaded that he was most anxious to get away to visit his children. Ironically, Julia's dislike of Mary Lincoln probably saved Grant's life and affected the course of history.

Leaving the White House, Grant was cheered by passersby who recognized him. Late that afternoon he and Julia left Washington by train. Meanwhile the papers, apprised earlier of Lincoln's planned invitation to the Grants, announced that Grant would share the President's box at Ford's Theater that evening for a performance of *Our American Cousin*.

When the Grants' train reached Philadelphia, he received the shocking news that the president had been assassinated at the theater. Secretary of State William Seward and his son had also been attacked.

"It would be impossible for me," Grant wrote, "to describe the feeling that overcame me at the news."

He was requested to return to Washington immediately with bodyguards, and to "keep close watch on all persons who come next to you in the cars." Julia was frightened.

"If we had gone to the theater with the president," she gasped, "you would have been killed, too!" She was probably right. It was learned that Grant's name had also been on the assassination list. Julia recalled that a lean, mustached, fierce-looking rider had galloped past the carriage that had taken them to the station, then had ridden back to stare at them again. Her description fit assassin John Wilkes Booth.

"This will make Andy Johnson president, will it not?" Julia asked her husband.

"Yes," he nodded, "and . . . I dread the change."

Johnson had been the only Southern senator, a Democrat, to support the Union in the Civil War. Grant knew that his attempt to carry out Lincoln's conciliatory Reconstruction policy in the South would clash with a Radical Republican Congress increasingly incensed by white Southerners' attempts to sabotage the civil rights of the emancipated slaves. Stormy days lay ahead.

Washington, which had been jubilant over Grant's victory, was now plunged into mourning for the president. But by May 23 victory parades marched through Washington in a two-day celebration, with Grant reviewing the troops.

The tremendous reception he received everywhere he went did not sit too well with Johnson. The new president saw Grant as a rival in the race for the White House in the next election. Johnson's chagrin increased as crowds chanted "Grant! Grant! Grant!" whenever he appeared at dinners or gatherings, even at a celebration to honor Johnson.

In July 1866 Congress voted to promote Grant to full General of the Armies of the United States, making him outrank even George Washington.

In the fall of 1867 Johnson, feuding with Stanton, suspended him as Secretary of War and appointed Grant temporarily in his place, hoping to derail Grant's presidential boom. Grant, uncomfortable at being moved into politics, accepted under protest. He remained at this post until January 1868, resigning promptly when Congress refused to permit Stanton's dismissal. The House of Representatives tried to impeach the president, but failed by one vote.

On May 20, 1868, Grant was nominated as the Republican candidate for president. Bored by politics, he hesitated to accept, but was finally persuaded to do so by powerful men around him. They saw in Grant a trusting, politically naive candidate they felt they could manipulate for their own profit.

"I shall have no policy of my own," Grant declared in his acceptance speech, "to interfere against the will of the people." His only indication of a goal for his administration was his invocation, "Let us have peace."

But if Grant wanted reconciliation between North and South, the Radicals dominating the Republican Party did not. They campaigned for him as the hero who had defeated the Confederacy.

Their posters proclaimed, "Vote As You Shot!"

When Grant won the election, Johnson was so embittered that he refused to ride in Grant's carriage to the inauguration, and absented himself from the ceremonies.

"The office has come to me unsought," Grant declared in his inaugural address. "I commence its duties untrammeled." As for Reconstruction, he urged that it "be approached calmly, without prejudice, hate, or sectional pride."

Grant's political enemies continued to portray him as a drunk, but when he became president he gave up drinking. His real weakness in the White House was that he was too easily impressed by rich men. They were the civilian successes he had aspired to be but never could. As president, Grant proved unwisely trusting, too naive, and a poor judge of character.

He actually knew nothing about politics, and had voted only once in his life in a presidential election. Pushed into the White House by a hero-worshipping public, he was probably one of the most poorly prepared presidents ever elected. He tried to learn the job as he went, but visitors observed that he looked like a man puzzled by the problems.

Once when he was asked if he liked Washington, Grant replied, "I'd like it better if it had a good road on which I could drive fast horses." He had new stables built on White House grounds in which he kept some spirited horses.

As First Lady, Julia became self-conscious about her appearance. She wanted an operation to correct a cast in one eye that led her to avoid being photographed head on. Grant persuaded her not to undergo it, declaring that he liked her crossed eyes and would not have her look any different.

Grant appointed questionable characters and relatives to important government jobs. Congress was incredulous when he included in his cabinet two friends from his hometown of Galena, and several men noted only for their wealth, some of whom had presented him with costly gifts.

During Grant's years as president, corrupt big business moguls manipulated some of Grant's officials to award their railroads subsidies and grants of free public land. Organizing monopolies, they raised commodity prices to consumers, and committed fraud on the stock market.

They also fooled Grant into ending peace treaties with the Indians. After he made the Indians "wards of the government," and confined them to reservation ghettos, land speculators seized mineral-rich Indian lands, making quick fortunes. Grant really wanted fairer treatment for the Indians, but allowed shrewd, wealthy businessmen to manipulate his policies.

When Grant's sister Virginia married Abel Corbin, a sixty-one-year-old New York financier, it set off a chain of events with disastrous consequences for Grant. Infamous speculators James Fisk and Jay Gould bribed Corbin for inside information from the White House. Planning to corner the gold market, the two stock market manipulators publicly entertained Grant on their yacht. Urging him not to release gold reserves from the Treasury, which could thwart their scheme, they believed they had persuaded him.

The naturalist John Burroughs observed that Grant "walked with men of money now." Historian Henry Adams said wryly, "A great soldier might be a baby politician."

Fisk and Gould secretly bought up all the gold stock they could, making it scarce and so driving up the price. Editor Horace Greeley exposed their swindle in his newspaper. Grant was shocked by exposure of their plot. He sought to thwart it by ordering the Treasury to sell four million dollars in gold, making it plentiful so that it drove down the value of the gold stock held by the speculators.

But the sharp drop in gold prices also created a panic on September 24, 1869 — "Black Friday." Many Wall Street brokers were ruined as the stock market plunged. Grant was blamed for his involvement with rich crooks.

Next year another Grant administration scandal erupted. The black-ruled island government of Santo Domingo (now the Dominican Republic) had asked Grant for annexation to the United States. He saw the offer as a possible solution to the Southern race problem.

"The emancipated race of the South," Grant wrote, "would have found there a congenial home, where their civil rights would not be disputed. . . . Thus in cases of great oppression and cruelty, such as has been practiced upon them in many places . . . whole communities would have sought refuge in Santo Domingo."

But in effect, this was a racist point of view, seeking to exile blacks from their American home. Lincoln had also endorsed this plan by supporting a movement to colonize Latin America by an emigration of American blacks.

With Grant's usual bad judgment, he sent two old friends to Santo Domingo to negotiate the deal. A Senate investigation discovered that they had been secretly promised valuable land on the island

if the annexation went through. They had also persuaded Grant to order United States navy vessels
to the island to prevent a revolt against Santo Domingo's president.

The Senate voted down the annexation.

A redeeming feature of Grant's first administration was his support for the Fifteenth Amendment
giving blacks the constitutional right to vote. It was
ratified on March 30, 1870.

He also demonstrated concern for Native Amer-
icans by appointing his Indian friend and former
war comrade, Ely Parker, as Indian commissioner.
Even though Grant's presidency was marked by
Indian warfare, he sought to pursue a peace policy.
He became the first president to invite Native
American chiefs like Red Cloud to the White House
to listen to their treaty grievances.

Under Grant, Reconstruction in the South was
carried out with Northern bayonets, primarily as a
result of policies enacted by Congress. Taking advantage of the North's military occupation of the
South, Northern businessmen and politicians went
South to gain control of the state governments,
making money by questionable means. The governments they controlled were known as "carpetbag" governments, named after the carpetbags or
traveling bags the transplanted Northerners carried.

Some carpetbaggers, however, were missionaries or abolitionists who honestly wanted to help the Freedmen's Bureau, which Congress had set up in the South in March 1865 to provide assistance to the newly emancipated Southern blacks.

The carpetbaggers' influx into the South, backed by Northern troops, did not make Grant popular with Southerners. In reprisal many joined the Ku Klux Klan and other racist societies.

Grant signed the Ku Klux Klan Act passed by Congress to enforce the Fourteenth Amendment, permitting the direct intervention of Northern troops in any Southern area where the Klan committed outrages. Southerners accused of racist crimes were no longer tried by Southern courts and juries, but by Federal courts. Under the act, 7,400 Southerners were indicted, although very few were convicted.

To appease the South before Election Day in 1872, Grant was persuaded by his advisors to abolish the Freedmen's Bureau, setting blacks adrift to make their own way with no further help.

Despite his troubled first term, Grant was easily reelected in a race against Democrat Horace Greeley. He somehow managed to seem untainted in voters' eyes. Blaming the betrayal of men who had taken advantage of him, Americans refused to relinquish their view of Grant as a noble war hero.

"I have been the subject of abuse and slander," Grant said at his second inaugural, "scarcely ever equalled in political history, which today I feel that

I can afford to disregard in view of your verdict, which I gratefully accept as my vindication."

But more bad news for Grant began in 1873 with a financial crisis that resulted in the longest depression the nation had ever experienced, lasting until 1879. He wanted to fight it by issuing more paper money not backed by gold, to let people pay off debts in cheaper money and buy more things to get the economy moving once again.

However, conservative wealthy businessmen and bankers, whose advice Grant respected, persuaded him to veto a popular "green-back law" passed by Congress to put more paper money in circulation. Grant's veto increased public resentment and brought on the financial panic of 1873.

Over the next years corruption was exposed in the Post Office, Treasury Department, Department of the Interior, and Navy Department. Worst of all, Grant's Secretary of War, General William W. Belknap, was discovered taking money from the sale of Western trading posts.

The public believed Grant to be personally honest, but naive, politically incompetent, and stubbornly loyal to the crooked men who surrounded him and took advantage of him. His poor business judgment was no surprise to those who had known him before the Civil War. But Grant was forgiven his shortcomings, at least in the North, because his image as the war hero persisted.

"Sure what's going on in Washington smells to high heaven," one New Yorker sighed. "But when hasn't it? Other presidents were just luckier that the crooks in their administrations got away with it, so the public never found out!"

Trouble piled on trouble. In 1875 Grant found himself faced with defiance by Southerners furious at the carpetbag state governments that had allowed blacks and Northerners to upset white domination. The Ku Klux Klan and other racist organizations led violent raids against Southern blacks.

Grant had no stomach for another bloody civil war. "I have no desire to have United States troops interfere in the domestic concerns of Louisiana or any other state," he declared. Instead he pressured Congress for passage of the Civil Rights Act of 1875. It guaranteed equal rights for blacks in public places, and forbade exclusion of blacks from jury duty. But without enforcement, the new act was sneered at by Southern racists.

In 1876 Grant tried to persuade the Sioux to accept 25,000 dollars for the right of miners and hunters to use their land. When the Sioux refused, Sherman granted General George Armstrong Custer a command in the Dakota Territory to fight the Sioux. Grant reluctantly gave his approval.

In a battle with Chief Crazy Horse on June 25, 1876, Custer and 260 cavalrymen were defeated and killed at Little Bighorn River. News of this greatest Native American victory increased dissatisfaction with Grant's continual blunders.

When Grant's second term expired, he apologized for his failure as president in his State of the Union message.

"It was my fortune, or misfortune, to be called to the office of Chief Executive without any previous political training," he said on December 5, 1876. "It is but reasonable to suppose that errors of judgment must have occurred. . . . Mistakes have been made, as all can see and I admit . . . oftener in the selections made of the assistants appointed to aid."

He told friends, "I never wanted to get out of a place as much as I did to get out of the presidency."

After surrendering the White House with relief to Rutherford B. Hayes, Grant and Julia began traveling around the world on a second honeymoon in the spring of 1877. If he left the presidency under a cloud, the rest of the world didn't seem to know it. Wherever the Grants went, they were received royally.

They dined with Queen Victoria at Windsor Castle, were received by the Emperor of Japan, the Russian czar, and the Pope. Banquets, parades, and cheering ovations honored their visits. Grant, who had once disliked and avoided ostentatious displays, now seemed to enjoy them. They were at least a welcome change from the bitter criticism he had endured during his eight years in the White House.

In India, at the palace of the Majarajah of Jaipur, Grant was invited on a tiger hunt safari. He turned it down.

"Twice in my life I killed wild animals," he told a Scottish duke, "and I have regretted both acts ever since."

Supporters who hoped to seek a third term for him urged Grant to stay abroad as long as possible, letting favorable publicity about his world trip dim memories of his administration.

"I am both homesick and dread going home," he wrote a friend. "I have no home but must establish one when I get back. Where I do not know."

The Grants finally returned to San Francisco in August 1879. Having been hailed around the world, Grant wondered what sort of a reception might now await him from his fellow Americans. He needn't have worried. Huge, enthusiastic crowds turned out to cheer his return.

Continuing to tour — the United States, Cuba, Mexico — the Grants received affectionate receptions everywhere. Apparently the scandals of his two administrations were at least forgiven, if not forgotten. The cheers and applause were primarily for General Grant, however, rather than for President Grant. This became clear when his name was placed in nomination for a third term at the Republican convention.

The nomination went to James Garfield instead. Money raised by wealthy friends allowed Grant to buy a mansion in New York City. Millionaire William Vanderbilt lent him 150,000 dollars to start a brokerage partnership. Running the American government hadn't increased Grant's business ability. In mid-1884 the firm suddenly failed when his partner falsified the books. Grant was again left penniless and humiliated by his inability to judge character or succeed in civilian life.

A lifesaving offer came from Mark Twain, who was a publisher as well as a famous author. He offered to publish Grant's memoirs, paying a generous 10,000 dollars and a percentage of sales of the book, which were to amount to over 420,000 dollars. Grant, elated for once at being successful at *something* in civilian life, set to work on his memoirs with a will.

Suffering an injury from a fall that confined him to the house, he did not let that keep him from working steadily on the book. But when he developed a cancer of the throat that was inoperable, Grant realized he was in a race with death.

He needed to finish the book because it would let him leave money to Julia, his children, and grandchildren. The civilian failure was determined to end his life, for once, with a successful venture.

He was assisted in his final endeavor by a former military aide, writer Adam Badeau.

Defying incessant pain, Grant forged ahead with the book, stubbornly refusing as always to turn aside from a goal he had set himself. When it was too painful for him to whisper dictation to Badeau, he scribbled himself. His pen now proved as mighty as his sword in battle.

As he struggled against time and cancer, Grant was visited by many friends, both Southern and Northern. He was touched to receive a letter of sympathy even from Jefferson Davis.

Almost finished with the memoirs, Grant wrote his doctor, "I am ready now to go at any time. I know there is nothing but suffering for me while I do live."

In June 1885 he was moved to a cottage at Mt. McGregor in the Adirondack foothills of New York State. Here he continued to be cared for tenderly by the ever-loyal Julia.

On June 16 Grant's *Personal Memoirs* was finished.

One week later, his last and only successful civilian endeavor accomplished, he was dead at age sixty-three. Grant had lived the same number of years as his once-great foe, Robert E. Lee.

A funeral cortege of generals and Civil War comrades, both Northern and Southern, proceeded behind his coffin as it moved down Fifth Avenue. Twelve years later a second cortege marked the dedication of the massive Grant's Tomb in New York City on the Hudson River. It bore the inscription of Grant's plaintive appeal at the close of the Civil War: "Let Us Have Peace."

The old warrior had his peace at last.

# Chronology

## 1860

| | |
|---|---|
| December 20, 1860 | South Carolina secedes |

## 1861

| | |
|---|---|
| April 12, 1861 | Fort Sumter fired upon |
| July 21, 1861 | First Battle of Bull Run (Manassas) |
| May 10, 1861–March 8, 1862 | Battle for Missouri |

## 1862

| | |
|---|---|
| February 6, 1862 | Capture of Fort Henry |
| February 13–16, 1862 | Capture of Fort Donelson |
| April 6–7, 1862 | Battle of Shiloh |
| June 26–July 1, 1862 | Seven Days' Battle |
| August 29–September 2, 1862 | Second Battle of Bull Run (Manassas) |
| September 17, 1862 | Battle of Antietam |
| September 13–October 13, 1862 | Capture of Iuka-Corinth |
| December 13, 1862 | Battle of Fredericksburg |
| December 27, 1862–July 22, 1863 | First Vicksburg Campaign |

## 1863

| | |
|---|---|
| April 27–May 4, 1863 | Battle of Chancellorsville |
| May 18–July 1, 1863 | Second Vicksburg Campaign |
| July 1–3, 1863 | Battle of Gettysburg |
| September 19–20, 1863 | Battle of Chickamauga |

## 1864

| | |
|---|---|
| May 6–7, 1864 | Battle of the Wilderness |
| May 8–12, 1864 | Battle of Spotsylvania |
| June 3, 1864 | Battle of Cold Harbor |
| June 14–August 25, 1864 | First Petersburg Campaign |
| July 30, 1864 | Battle of the Crater |
| September 2–December 20, 1864 | Sherman's March Through Georgia |

## 1865

| | |
|---|---|
| March 25–April 2, 1865 | Second Petersburg Campaign |
| April 3, 1865 | Fall of Richmond |
| April 9, 1865 | Surrender at Appomattox |

# Bibliography

Anderson, Nancy Scott. *The Generals — Ulysses S. Grant and Robert E. Lee.* New York: Knopf, 1987.

Archer, Jules. *Indian Foe, Indian Friend.* New York: Crowell-Collier Press, 1970.

Bains, Rae. *Robert E. Lee: Brave Leader.* New Jersey: Troll Associates, 1986.

Brandt, Keith. *Robert E. Lee.* New Jersey: Troll Associates, 1985.

Cadwallader, Sylvanus. *Three Years With Grant.* New York: Knopf, 1961.

Carter, Hodding. *Robert E. Lee and the Road of Honor.* New York: Random House, 1955.

Catton, Bruce. *A Stillness At Appomattox.* New York: Washington Square Press, 1958.

———. *Never Call Retreat.* New York: Washington Square Press, 1967.

———. *Reflections On the Civil War.* New York: Berkley Books, 1981.

———. *Terrible Swift Sword.* New York: Washington Square Press, 1967.

Commager, Henry Steele. *America's Robert E. Lee.* Boston: Houghton Mifflin, 1951.

Daniels, Jonathon. *Robert E. Lee*. Boston: Houghton Mifflin, 1960.

Davis, Burke. *Gray Fox: Robert E. Lee and the Civil War*. New York: Rinehart, 1956.

Dowdey, Clifford. *Lee*. Boston: Little, Brown, 1965.

Duboswski, Cathy East. *Robert E. Lee and the Rise of the South*. Englewood Cliffs, N.J.: Silver Burdett Press, 1991.

Fishwick, Marshall William. *Lee After the War*. New York: Dodd, Mead, 1963.

Flood, Charles Bracelen. *Lee: The Last Years*. Boston: Houghton Mifflin, 1981.

Freeman, Douglas Southall. *R.E. Lee*. New York/London: Charles Scribner's Sons, 1934.

Frost, Lawrence A. *U.S. Grant Album*. Seattle: Superior Publishing Co., 1966.

Fuller, Maj. Gen. J.F.C. *Grant and Lee*. Bloomington: Indiana University Press, 1957.

Grant, Matthew G. *Ulysses S. Grant: General and President*. Chicago: Childrens Press, 1974.

Grant, Ulysses S. *Personal Memoirs*. New York: Da Capo Press, Inc., 1952.

Greene, Carol. *Robert E. Lee: Leader in War and Peace*. Chicago: Children's Press, 1989.

Hansen, Harry. *The Civil War: A History*. New York: New American Library, 1961.

Jones, J. William. *Personal Reminiscences, Anecdotes and Letters of Gen. Robert E. Lee*. New York: D. Appleton, 1875.

Lee, Robert E. *Recollections and Letters*. Garden City, N.Y.: Doubleday & Company, Inc., 1924.

Lewis, Lloyd. *Captain Sam Grant*. Boston: Little, Brown, 1950.

Marshall, Charles. *An Aide-de-camp of Lee*. Boston: Little, Brown, 1927.

McFeely, William S. *Grant*. New York/London: W.W. Norton & Company, 1981.

Miers, Earl Schenck. *The Web of Victory: Grant at Vicksburg*. New York: Knopf, 1955.

National Park Service. *Arlington House*. Washington, D.C.: U.S. Department of the Interior, 1985.

Nolan, Alan T. *Lee Considered*. Chapel Hill: University of North Carolina Press, 1991.

Page, Thomas Nelson. *Robert E. Lee: Man and Soldier*. New York: Charles Scribner's Sons, 1911.

Sanborn, Margaret. *Robert E. Lee*. Philadelphia: Lippincott, 1966.

Sinkler, George. *The Racial Attitudes of American Presidents*. Garden City, N.Y.: Doubleday & Company, Inc., 1971.

Smith, Gene. *Lee and Grant*. New York: McGraw Hill, 1984.

Stern, Philip Van Doren. *Robert E. Lee: The Man and Soldier*. New York: Bonanza Books, 1963.

Thomas, Henry. *Ulysses S. Grant*. New York: Putnam, 1961.

Todd, Helen. *A Man Named Grant.* Boston: Houghton Mifflin, 1940.

Weidhorn, Manfred. *Robert E. Lee.* New York: Atheneum, 1988.

Woodward, William E. *Meet General Grant.* Literary Guild of America, 1928.

# Index

# Index

childhood of, 5, 11–14

civilians and, 74–75

Cold Harbor, Battle of, 119–120

command style of, 43–44, 45, 58, 59–60, 94

commissioned brigadier general, 50

Crater, Battle of, 125–126

death of, 171–172

drinking and, 33, 34–35, 44, 50, 54, 62, 68–69, 102, 108, 160

education of, 12–13, 14–16

elected president, 160

health of, 132, 142, 170, 171

injury at New Orleans, 100

Kentucky campaign of, 50–51

Lee and, 103–104, 112–114, 125, 136–137, 152, 155–156

Lee surrenders to, 139–149

Lincoln and, 68–69, 102, 112, 121, 127, 130–131

marriage of, to Julia Dent, 17, 32–33

McClernand and, 80–81

memoirs of, 170–171

Mexican War opposed by, 17–18

military postings of, 16–17, 33

Missouri campaign, 46–47

personality and demeanor of, 11, 13–14, 16, 104, 106, 109

politics and, 102–103, 107–108, 128

presidency of, 160–168

prisoner exchanges and, 111

promoted General of the Armies, 159

promoted lieutenant-general, 106, 107

promoted major general, 61, 99

public adulation of, 106–107, 157, 159, 169

reelection of, 165–166

resigns from Army, 34–35

Richmond, advance on, 121–122, 123

Shiloh, Battle of, 64–69

slavery opposed by, 53–54

Spotsylvania, Battle of, 115–117, 118

Tennessee campaign of, 58–63

Vicksburg campaign, 84–85, 90, 94–99

Wilderness campaign, 114–115

Grant, Virginia Paine (sister), 13, 162

Greeley, Horace, 162, 165

Halleck, Henry Wagner, 118

civilians and, 74–75

Grant and, 53, 54, 58, 59, 60, 61–63, 69–70, 74, 80–81, 84

Vicksburg siege and, 95, 96

Harris, Thomas, 46, 47

Hayes, Rutherford B., 121, 168

Hill, A. P., 58, 73

Hill, Benjamin, 129–130

Hood, John B., 79, 129

Hooker, Joseph ("Fighting Joe")

Chancellorsville, Battle of, 86–89

replacement of, 90

Jackson, Thomas ("Stonewall"), 42, 70–71

Bull Run (Manassas), Battle of, 48–49, 76

Chancellorsville, Battle of, 87, 88

Johnson, Andrew, 151, 152, 155, 160

impeachment effort, 159

presidency, 158, 159

Johnston, Albert, 64, 66

Johnston, Joe, 6, 57, 133, 137, 138, 139, 140

Ku Klux Klan, 165, 167

*181*

# Index

Lee, Anne Hill Carter (mother), 1, 3, 4, 6–7
Lee, Annie (daughter), 82
Lee, Curtis (son), 10, 20, 23, 150
Lee, Henry (father), 1–2, 3, 8, 27, 44
Lee, Mary Custis (wife), 20, 21, 43, 49, 55, 56, 72, 74, 78, 86, 101, 124–125, 132
 health of, 150, 151
 marriage of, 7–9
Lee, Mary (daughter), 152
Lee, Mildred (daughter), 155
Lee, Robert E., 11, 38, 171
 amnesty granted to, 155
 appointed commander-in-chief of Confederate Army, 64
 atrocities and, 75
 birth of, 1
 Bull Run (Manassas), Battle of
 first, 49
 second, 75–77
 Chancellorsville, Battle of, 86–89
 childhood of, 1–4
 coastal defenses and, 55–56
 Cold Harbor, Battle of, 119–120
 command of Virginia's military accepted by, 42
 command style of, 43, 44, 56–57, 73–74, 80
 Crater, Battle of, 125–126
 criticism of, 129–130
 Davis and, 43, 55, 108, 117, 118, 138
 death of, 156
 desertions and, 99–100, 133–134
 education of, 4–7, 16
 entrenchment strategy of, 56
 finances of, 7, 150, 152
 Fort Carrol construction, 22–23
 Fredericksburg, Battle of, 82–83
 Gettysburg, Battle of, 68, 90–93
 Grant and, 31, 103–104, 109–110, 112–114, 125, 136–137, 155–156
 health of, 86, 100–101, 150
 Indian wars and, 23–24
 indictment for treason, 150, 151
 John Brown's raid and, 25–26
 marriage of, to Mary Custis, 7–9
 Maryland campaign of, 77–79
 Mexican War experience of, 19–22, 56
 Mexican War opposed by, 19
 military postings of, 8–10
 Northern army command offered to, 39
 personality and demeanor of, 3, 6, 9, 21, 22
 Petersburg siege and, 132–133, 138–139
 Reconstruction and, 153–154
 resigns from Army (U.S.), 40
 Richmond defense, 71
 Seven Days' Battle, 73–74
 Shiloh, Battle of, 67
 slavery and, 24, 25, 27, 39
 Spotsylvania, Battle of, 115–117
 surrender of, 139–149
 Virginia secession and, 27–28
 Washington College presidency, 152–153, 154–155
 West Point administration and, 10, 23
 Wilderness campaign, 114–115
 women and, 6, 10
Lee, Robert E., Jr. (son), 72, 76, 150
Lee, Rooney (son), 72, 100–101, 150
Lincoln, Abraham, 5, 39, 118
 armistice possibilities, 133, 134
 assassination of, 157–158, 159
 Chancellorsville, Battle of, 88
 Civil War and, 38, 41, 70, 77, 90, 93, 108, 123, 127, 138
 Cold Harbor, Battle of, 120
 Davis, Jefferson and, 92–93

# Index

elected president, 26
election of 1864, 105, 111, 120–
121, 130–131
Gettysburg Address, 102
Grant and, 61, 62, 68–69, 85,
90, 99, 101, 102, 103, 104–
105, 107, 108, 112, 121,
132
Halleck and, 63
Hooker and, 85–86
McClernand and, 80
Mexican War opposed by, 17
reelection of, 130–131
Longstreet, James, 109, 113

Manassas, Battle of (Battle of Bull
Run)
first, 48–50
second, 75–77
Marshall, Charles, 57, 88, 142
McClelland, George B., 15, 33, 44,
55, 72
Antietam Creek, Battle of, 79
Army of the Potomac command,
53, 70, 82
Bull Run (Manassas), Battle of,
75
Grant and, 59
Halleck and, 62
politics and, 120–121
Richmond offensive, 71, 73
Washington defense, 77, 78
McClernand, John, 69
Grant and, 80–81
relieved from command, 96
Vicksburg campaign, 84
McLean, Wilmer, 143
Meade, George M., 109, 116, 142
Gettysburg, Battle of, 90–93
Lee and, 110, 111
Wilderness campaign, 114
Mexican War, 46
Grant opposes, 17–18
Grant's experience in, 29–32
Lee opposes, 19

Lee's experience in, 19–22
treaty provisions ending, 22
Mosby, John S., 114

New York City, draft riots in, 93–
94

Petersburg, Virginia
fall of, 138–139
siege of, 121–122, 123, 124,
125, 127–128, 129, 130,
132, 133
Pickett, George, 91–92
Pope, John, 62, 75, 76
Prisoners of war
camps for, 111–112, 124
exchanges of, Grant and, 111
surrender terms and, 146

Rawlins, John A., 41, 50, 108
Reconstruction
Grant and, 160, 164–165
Johnson and, 158
Lee and, 153–154
Richmond, Virginia
advance on, 118–120, 121, 125
attack on, 110
defense of, 64, 71, 103–104,
112–113, 116, 117, 133
fall of, 139

Savannah, Georgia, fall of, 131–
132
Scott, Winfield
Civil War experience of, 48, 52–
53
Lee and, 10, 23, 28, 39
Mexican War experience of, 20–
21, 22, 31
Seven Days' Battle, 73–74
Sheridan, Phil, 123, 127, 129, 138,
139, 140, 144
Sherman, William Tecumseh, 15
appointed head of cavalry, 108
Atlanta taken by, 128–129, 131

*183*

# Index